Azarmidokht Abazari
Leila Mehrdana
Mohammad Harooni Arani

Customer Relationship Management in Companies

Azarmidokht Abazari
Leila Mehrdana
Mohammad Harooni Arani

Customer Relationship Management in Companies

Noor Publishing

Imprint
Any brand names and product names mentioned in this book are subject to trademark, brand or patent protection and are trademarks or registered trademarks of their respective holders. The use of brand names, product names, common names, trade names, product descriptions etc. even without a particular marking in this work is in no way to be construed to mean that such names may be regarded as unrestricted in respect of trademark and brand protection legislation and could thus be used by anyone.

Cover image: www.ingimage.com

Publisher:
Noor Publishing
is a trademark of
Dodo Books Indian Ocean Ltd., member of the OmniScriptum S.R.L Publishing group
str. A.Russo 15, of. 61, Chisinau-2068, Republic of Moldova Europe
Printed at: see last page
ISBN: 978-620-3-85874-7

Customer Relationship Management in Companies

By

Dr. Azarmidokht Abazari

PhD in Public Management Majoring in Human Resources, Islamic Azad University, Astara Branch, Astara, Iran

Leila Mehrdana

Graduate of Health Care Management, Islamic Azad University, North Tehran Branch, Tehran, Iran

Mohammad Harooni Arani

Master of Business Administration in E-Commerce, Islamic Azad University, Rudbar Branch, Rudbar, Iran

Dr. Azarmidokht Abazari

PhD in Public Management Majoring in Human Resources,
Islamic Azad University, Astara Branch, Astara, Iran

Leila Mehrdana

Graduate of Health Care Management, Islamic Azad University,
North Tehran Branch, Tehran, Iran

Mohammad Harooni Arani

Master of Business Administration in E-Commerce, Islamic Azad
University, Rudbar Branch, Rudbar, Iran

This Book is dedicated to

My Family's

Content

Chapter I

Introduction

Introduction

Supply chain management is one of the basic pillars in any supply chain and plays a very vital role in the survival and continuity of successful supply chain operations in the global competitive market. Many variables play a role in the successful performance of supply chain management, but the most important element in today's business is the identification of customer needs and wants by the customer relationship management system. Management efforts to achieve business unit goals based on dual program tasks Planning and control are established.

The task of planning is basically a decision-making process that deals with issues such as determining the expected profit, supply and access to raw materials, labor and machinery, estimating production volume and creating an internal and external communication system. .... deals with; The control task is to organize and combine natural resources, labor and production tools in a coordinated unit to achieve the desired results. Makes secondary control possible (Milton, 1996).

Nowadays, various products should be made available to the customer according to his request; Customer demand for high quality and fast service has increased pressures that did not exist before, so companies can no longer do everything on their own, although all industrial accounting systems in the organization are necessary, but in existing competitive market in addition to dealing with the organization and internal resources, economic and manufacturing enterprises have also found themselves in the need to manage and monitor related resources and elements outside the organization.

Accordingly, activities such as supply and demand planning, production of raw materials and product planning, product maintenance service, inventory control, distribution, delivery and customer service, which were previously performed at the company level, are now transferred to the supply chain level.

The key issue in a supply chain is the coordinated management and control of all these activities. Supply chain management is a phenomenon that does this in a way that customers can find reliable and fast service with quality products at the lowest cost (Wajdi Wahid, 2007).

Managers are more responsible than ever for directing limited resources and achieving the highest results, given the difficult conditions of the current economy. In this regard, decision-making centers, to guide and allocate resources, need support systems that supply chain management can be a system that provides valuable assistance to managers across the chain. Supply chains connect suppliers to a manufacturing company and the company to its customers.

Proper supply chain management is essential to ensure excellent customer service, low costs and short cycle times. There are several types of supply chains, the most important of which are "integrated fabrication for storage", "continuous filling after unloading", "custom-made fabrication" and "channel assembly". Supply chain management is difficult despite the uncertainty in supply and demand and the need for coordination between several partners' business activities. Information technology has also taken an effective step in solving the mentioned problems by supporting the proposed solutions, including software (supply chain management), customer relationship management, capital resource planning, optimal production technology, as well as evolved modes.

And integrated supply chain management and customer relationship management. The second form of IT supply assistance is through the e-commerce function, which is provided by automating processes and integrating core business activities through an electronic structure. But order execution in e-commerce is also very difficult for customers due to the need to carry small packages of goods, which can be solved through solutions such as same-day delivery and even the same time and automatic warehouses.

Statement of the problem

The success of many private, governmental and military organizations depends on their ability to deliver approved outputs. Provide better products in a wide range with low cost and fast delivery. Optimal delivery of these outputs (cost, quality, performance, delivery, flexibility and innovation) depends on the organization's ability to manage the flow of materials, information and money inside and outside the organization. This flow is known as the supply chain. Problems arise because supply chains can be long and complex and involve a large number of business partners. These problems can lead to customer dissatisfaction and loss of sales in the event of delays, and incur high costs for the organization to bear. Many world-class companies attribute much of their success to supply chain management, which is widely supported by customer relationship management (Figure 1).

Globalization and technological advancement have led to close competition between companies, and in the competitive arena, successful units will be able to compete with other competitors, which requires more focus on customer needs and meeting their expectations. Today's business is not only about development and improvement, delivery and sales, but also maintains long-term relationships with customers. One of the major advances in business today is to increase profits and productivity as a result of customer satisfaction and improve supply chain management, so that if business units focus on new customers, more customer retention and increased time cycle value.

Figure 1. Impact of Technology on Globalization

In other words, a business that does not meet customer expectations and does not have a stable and dynamic relationship with customers in the long run, will disappear from the global competition in the long run. Nowadays, the way of interactions between organizations has changed. These rapid changes in the global environment with high demand and reciprocal supply are abundant, which companies must be able to quickly integrate with the new position of customer relationship management and supply chain management to meet today's market.

Since no research has been done on the interrelationship between supply chain management and customer relationship management, so it is necessary to fill the existing study gap by doing this research and ultimately enrich the existing scientific resources in the field. Also, conducting such research will identify the interrelationships of different dimensions of supply chain management and customer relationship management in the company and ultimately will lead to greater productivity in the company.

Customer relation management

Systems are said to collect information from customers and analyze their needs, and in customer relationship management, customer relationship management system or the result of providing a suitable solution to improve the business relationship with customers through new means of communication (Figure 2).

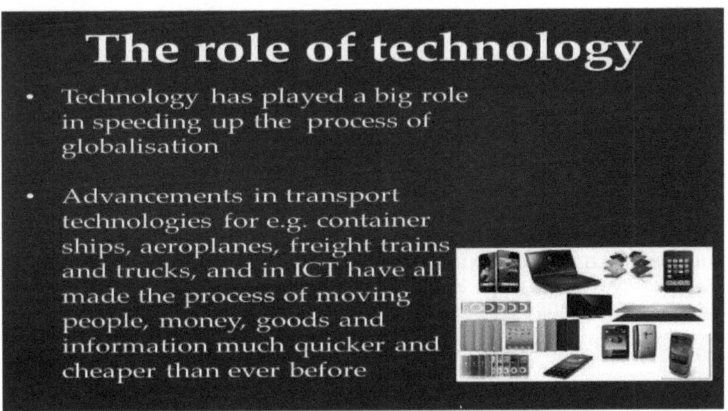

Figure 2. Globalization. The role of technology

Operational definitions of variables

Efficiency: Comparing the output obtained with the consumed inputs determines the efficiency. For example, reducing the cost of providing human resources, the cost of using equipment, creating high turnover and minimizing inventory.

Integration: Integration means the existence of a comprehensive process (sectoral and extra-sectoral) that works on functional and non-functional activities in the direction of strategic goals of the organization using interconnected, interactive and flexible organizational structures. Due to the integration of technologies, People functions, management knowledge and science, business processes, communications and organizational interactions are fully integrated and operate continuously. For example, the existence of multitasking integration to operate activities, facilitate simultaneous operations, follow a single administrative and operational policies and procedures.

Accountability: Accountability for actions taken and the ability to meet the expectations of customers and individuals or legal entities against whom a task is expected. For example, the ability to respond quickly to unforeseen demand or the ability to meet customer expectations and demands.

Trust: This means that the company's willingness to take risks in relation to other companies, for example risk taking, may lead to credibility and gain the trust of other companies.

Customer care

Customer care involves creating systems to maximize customer satisfaction in the business. Such as paying attention to customer needs, providing high quality services to customers, the importance of customer satisfaction for the company.

Understand the needs of customers

Understanding customer needs is the most important step in the sales process and is the company's scientific effort to identify the types of important customer needs that the company can meet those needs. For example, recognizing the type of consumer needs of its customers, as well as recognizing the level of customer interest in the company's products, awareness of customer satisfaction with the quality of goods or needs assessment of the type of goods preferred by customers.

Chapter II

Research Literature

Introduction

With the passage of the traditional economy and the intensification of competition in new dimensions, the customer as someone who the organization wants to influence his behavior with the values it creates, has become the main pillar and axis of all activities of organizations, so that from a competitive perspective, the survival and continuity of organizations is expressed in the group of identifying and attracting new customers and retaining existing customers. On the other hand, the development of communication, the evolution of the information age, and the emergence of new communication tools, organizations with a large number of different customers, they are faced with many options that result in more customer control and market instability.

Management and marketing have prescribed the version of customer retention and the right ways to communicate with them under the title of customer relationship management, which has been seriously introduced by Tom Sell since 1993 and entered the public sphere. In its simplest terms, customer relationship management is putting the customer at the heart of the business and the highest degree of importance.

In our country, although with delays in the global economy, in recent years, customerism issues have opened their place in relations between people with organizations and government relations with people, and the need to pay attention and satisfy the needs and desires of customers in a serious way. The course of rapid developments and changes in the current competitive market has led organizations to pay more attention to the systems that affect the progress of the organization's activities in order to overcome competitors.

One of the systems that can have a significant impact on the decisions of the organization is customer relationship management. Customer relationship management, collects information based on current and future needs and wants of customers. The comprehensive and codified information that customer relationship management provides to supply chain management is a decision-making strategy for estimating customer needs and a step towards designing an organization around customers. This chapter reviews the research literature on supply chain management and management. Will have a relationship with the customer.

Therefore, this chapter is divided into two parts, the first part is the research literature on supply chain management and the second part will be the literature on customer relationship management and finally a review of foreign and domestic research on the subject of the present study.

Supply Chain Management

Today, supply chain management is considered as one of the infrastructure foundations of e-business implementation in the world. In the current global competition, various products should be made available to the customer according to his request. Customer demand for high quality and fast service has increased pressures that did not exist before, as a result of which companies can no longer do everything on their own.

In the existing competitive market, economic and manufacturing enterprises, in addition to dealing with the organization and internal resources, have found themselves in need of managing and monitoring related resources and elements outside the organization. The reason for this is to gain a competitive advantage or advantages in order to gain more market share.

Accordingly, activities such as supply and demand planning, supply of materials, production and product planning, product maintenance service, inventory control, distribution, delivery and customer service, which were previously performed at the company level, have now been transferred to the supply chain level. The key issue in a supply chain is the coordinated management and control of all these activities. Supply chain management is a phenomenon that does this in such a way that customers can receive reliable and fast service with quality products at the lowest cost. In general, the supply chain consists of two or more organizations that are officially separated from each other. And are related to each other by material flows, information and financial flows (Jafarnejad, 2010, 8).

History of supply chain management

In the 1960s and 1970s, organizations sought to increase their competitiveness by standardizing and improving their internal processes to produce better quality and lower cost products. The prevailing thinking at the time was that strong engineering and design, as well as coherent production operations, were a prerequisite for achieving market demands and thus gaining more market share. For this reason, organizations focused all their efforts on increasing efficiency.

In the 1980s, as diversity in customer-expected patterns increased, organizations became increasingly interested in increasing flexibility in product lines and developing new products to meet customer needs. In the 1990s, along with improvements in production processes and the application of reengineering models, managers in many industries realized that not only improved internal processes and flexibility in the company's capabilities were sufficient to maintain market presence, but also suppliers of parts and materials. Produce quality and the lowest cost, and product distributors must also be closely associated with producer market development policies; With such an attitude, supply chain approaches and management emerged. On the other hand, with the rapid development of information technology in recent years and its widespread application in supply chain management, many basic activities of chain management are being carried out with new methods (Pouya, 2005, 21).

Definition of supply chain management

Brief and comprehensive definitions that can be provided of supply chain and supply chain management are: Supply chain includes all activities related to the flow and conversion of goods from the raw material stage (extraction) to delivery to the final consumer and related information flows . In general, the supply chain is a chain that includes all activities related to the flow of goods and the conversion of materials, from the stage of preparation of the raw material to the stage of delivery of the final product to the consumer. About the flow of goods There are two other flows, one is the flow of information and the other is the flow of financial resources and credits. (Ladon and Ladon, 14, 2002).

Supply chain management involves the integration of supply chain activities as well as related information flows through the improvement of chain relationships in order to achieve a reliable and sustainable competitive advantage. Therefore, supply chain management is the process of integrating supply chain activities as well as related information flows by improving and coordinating activities in the supply chain of production and product supply.

And distribution channels should be considered. The definition provided for the supply chain includes information systems management, sourcing and procurement, production scheduling, order processing, inventory management, warehousing, and customer service. For effective supply chain management, it is essential that suppliers and customers work with each other in a coordinated manner and through partnerships, information communications, and dialogue.

This means the rapid flow of information between customers and suppliers, distribution centers and transportation systems, enabling some companies to create highly efficient supply chains. Suppliers and customers must have the same goals; Suppliers and customers must trust each other. Customers trust their suppliers in the quality of products and services.

In addition, suppliers and customers must share in designing the supply chain to achieve common goals and facilitate communication and information flow. Some companies try to gain control of their supply chain with vertical general control and by using the ownership and integration of all the various components along the supply chain from the provision of materials and services to the delivery of the final product and customer service. But even with this type of organizational structure, different activities and operational units may be inconsistent. The organizational structure of the company should focus on coordinating different activities to achieve the overall goals of the company (Ibid., 17).

Value chain, supply and demand

Supply chains are sometimes referred to as value chains, a term that reflects such a concept: As goods and services evolve and move forward through the chain, their value increases. Supply or value chains usually involve separate business organizations rather than just one organization. In addition, the value supply chain for each organization has two parts: a supply part and a demand part.

The supply part starts from the beginning of the chain (beginning of the chain) and ends with the internal operations of the organization. The demand side of the chain starts at the point where the organization's output is delivered to the immediate customer and ends with the final customer in the chain. The demand chain is the sales and distribution sector in the value chain.

The length and size of each segment depends on where a particular organization is in the chain; The closer the organization is to the end customer, the shorter the demand side, and the longer the supply side. Figure 1-2 shows these concepts: All organizations, regardless of where they are in the chain, must deal with supply and demand issues. The goal of supply chain management is to connect all parts of the supply chain (supply) so that market demand is met as efficiently and effectively as possible throughout the chain. This requires matching supply and demand at each stage of the chain. Note that with the exception of the primary supplier or suppliers and final customers, organizations in a supply chain are both customer and supplier (Figure 3) (Ghazanfari et al., 2001, 27).

Figure 3. Globalization

Need for supply chain management

In the past, most organizations were less likely to manage their own supply chains. Instead, they tended to focus on their own operations and on their own immediate suppliers. However, several factors make supply chain management desirable for business organizations that actively manage their supply chain. The main factors are:

Need to improve operations: Over the past decade, many organizations have engaged in activities such as lean manufacturing and total quality management. As a result, they will be able to achieve improved quality while eliminating a large amount of extra costs outside of their system.

Although there is still room for improvement. Opportunity now exists mainly in procurement, distribution and support - supply chain. Increasing the level of external sourcing: Organizations are increasing the level of external sourcing; It means purchasing goods and services instead of producing or providing them by the organizations themselves. As the level of outsourcing increases, organizations are a large part of an organization and its suppliers.

This task is to obtain goods or services that are used to produce products or provide services to the organization's customers. Selects purchasing suppliers, negotiates contracts, forms alliances, and acts as a link between suppliers and various domestic departments. Purchasing has become increasingly important in supply chain management. Several factors contribute to this:

Increased external sourcing: The point is that the cost of materials and supplies is much higher than the cost of labor. Increased conversion to lean manufacturing and JIT requirements, which means smaller batch sizes, the need for accurate delivery schedules, higher quality, and accurate and complete quantities.

Increasing globalization: The supply chain of a supply chain (value) consists of one or more suppliers, all of which are interconnected in the chain, and each is able to influence the effectiveness - or ineffectiveness - of the supply chain. In addition, it is essential that planning and execution are carefully coordinated between suppliers and all members of their demand side.

Proximity to the market or proximity to supply sources, or proximity to both may be possible. In total quality management, reference is made to benchmarking, that is, evaluating the current position of the company and using it as a guide for the position that the company wants to be in the future. However, a company must evaluate performance and set overall goals in terms of the entire supply chain, not just the company alone (Pouya, 2005, 44).

A company may set high goals for itself to minimize inventory, but if the inventory levels of the company's suppliers need to be high so that the company can achieve its local goals regardless of the suppliers' costs, then the inventory cost. The above is considered higher for the company as parts delivery costs and material costs.

If a company achieves its quality goals and ignores the quality plans of its suppliers, then inversely they will be able to deliver quickly to customers and replenish inventory through suppliers. If everyone with the supply chain gets the same information at the same time, it enables them to coordinate accurately, thus reducing uncertainty, which in turn allows them to reduce inventory levels. (Cohen et al., 2000, 1999)

The types and number of facilities and facilities that are built (or acquired) and the place where they are placed are among the topics of strategic design of the supply chain. Because transportation and distribution costs can make up a significant portion of supply chain costs, decisions about facilities and their location are costly and long-term commitments, as well as other design decisions such as Which suppliers dictate the process, method of transportation, distribution centers and customer markets. For example, 75% of Honda suppliers are located 150 miles from the Ohio, Wiresville plant. Wal-Mart is an example that has integrated these various design features into a successful and effective supply chain. Wal-Mart Competitive Strategy The supply of quality goods to its customers at the time and place they want, and at a competitive price (ibid., P. 79) is the key to achieving these strategic goals. They arrive at the warehouse from a supplier, are loaded from the supplier truck, and are loaded onto outbound or outbound trucks, thus avoiding storage and warehousing. They are delivered on a continuous basis and distributed to stores without being in stock. Goods pass from one dock loading to another dock load within 48 hours or less. This system allows Wal-Mart to buy full trucks full of goods, while also avoiding transportation and inventory costs (ibid., 80).

Performance criteria

It is important to evaluate and track supply chain performance, especially since several organizations are involved in the chain. A variety of criteria can be used for this purpose. One approach is to use the supply chain operations reference model, which is an attempt to standardize the supply chain performance evaluation.

Measurement criteria are:

- ✓ Timely delivery;
- ✓ Delivery time to fulfill the order;
- ✓ Filling rate (demand deficit that is met from inventory);
- ✓ Complete order fulfillment;
- ✓ Supply chain response time;
- ✓ Production flexibility;
- ✓ Cost of supply chain management;
- ✓ Guarantee cost as a percentage of revenue;
- ✓ Value added of each employee;
- ✓ Total available supply days;
- ✓ Box-to-box cycle time;
- ✓ Net asset transfer rate.

A conceptual framework

Supply chain management, as it operates today, has its origins in marketing, support, and production. These three dimensions are:

I.   In-house coordination (managing activities and processes within a company's support task);

II. Coordination of interoperable activities (such as coordination between support and finance, support and production, and support and marketing) as they take place within the company's operational areas; And

III. The coordination of inter-organizational supply chain activities that take place between legally separate companies within a product flow channel, such as between a company and its suppliers.

A distinct factor between each of these dimensions is the amount of control that the manager has over the flow of the product to achieve coordination (Jafarnejad, 2000, 36). That there is a means to manage the coalition. In order for the alliance to remain intact, the rewards of cooperation must be redistributed. This requires doing three things:

I. A new type of measurement tool beyond the usual accounting procedures for incorporating inter-organizational data and expressing it in terms that facilitate the analysis of benefits.

II. An information-sharing mechanism for transmitting information about the benefits associated with sharing efforts among channel members.

III. An allocation method for redistributing cooperation rewards in a way that benefits all sectors fairly.

New competition

Supply chain management represents a paradigm shift that increases the company's enthusiasm for the concepts of collaboration and competition. Collaboration does not seem to be a process between a set of exchanging partners.

Cooperation now exists throughout the supply chain. The basic premise of the new competition is that companies will not compete as long as they once did. The new global networking competition is centered on agile companies with managers who actively seek out different interpretations of events and are eager to think differently about their business, and respond quickly to market changes. (Blington et al., 1992, 48).

Collaboration and joint efforts

Without the needs of new competition, drastic changes and transformations take place between business partners. Our partnership, in which companies exchange some essential information and use some contracts or long-term supplier / customer contacts, is a threshold level of engagement. That is, cooperation is the starting point in supply chain management and is a necessary but insufficient condition. The next level is coordination, whereby both workflows and information are exchanged in a way that integrates EDI, JIT systems, and other mechanisms that seek to integrate many traditional relationships between and within business segments. It is possible. Businesses can work together to coordinate some activities, but they do not yet act as real partners. Again, this evolution is a necessary but insufficient condition for supply chain management (Heid and John, 1990, 15).

Supply chain management is built on trust and commitment. The consensus is that trust and confidence can significantly contribute to the long-term stability of an organization. Trust is expressed by faith, reliance, belief, or trust in the supply partner, and trust is simply the belief in the company that the supply chain partner of the company will act consistently and that what the company says it will do, the partner will do. gives. Commitment is the belief that business partners are willing to devote energy to maintaining this relationship. That is, through the commitment of committed partners, resources are allocated to maintain and achieve the goals of the supply chain. Supply chain partners, for example, are reluctant to share information about future plans and programs, as well as information about competitive forces and R&D. Partners recognize that their long-term success depends on the strength of their weakest supply chain partner. Is. Figure 4 summarizes the necessary transitions from an important supplier to a supply chain partner (Cross, 2000, 32).

The overall layout of a supply chain

In general, supply chain is a chain that includes all activities related to the flow of goods and conversion of materials, from the stage of preparation of the raw material to the stage of delivery of the final product to the consumer. In connection with the flow of goods, there are two other flows, one is the flow of information and the other is the flow of financial resources and credits.

Different researchers and writers have come up with different approaches and definitions of the supply chain. Some have limited the supply chain in the buyer-seller relationship, with such an approach focusing only on the first-tier purchasing operations in an organization.

Another group gives a broader perspective to the supply chain and considers it to include all sources of supply (supply bases) for the organization. According to this definition, the supply chain will include all first, second, third, etc. suppliers. Such an approach to the supply chain will only analyze the supply chain. The third view is Porter's value chain approach, in which the supply chain includes all the activities needed to deliver a product or service to the end customer. With this approach to the supply chain, manufacturing and distribution functions are added to the supply chain as part of the flow of goods and services; In fact, with this view, the supply chain includes three areas of supply, production and distribution (Holg et al., 2000,58).

Major supply chain management processes

Supply chain management has three main processes, which are:

1- Information management
2- Logistics management
3- Relationship management

Information Management: Today, the role, importance and position of information is obvious to everyone. Proper flow and proper transfer of information make processes more efficient and effective and easier to manage. In the supply chain discussion - as mentioned - the importance of coordination in activities is very important. This is also true in the discussion of information management in the chain, information systems management and information transfer. Coordinated and appropriate information management between partners will lead to increasing impacts on speed, accuracy, quality and other aspects. Proper information management will lead to more coordination in the chain. In general, in the supply chain, information management will be effective in various sectors, some of which are:

Logistics management (transfer, handling, processing, and access to logistics information to integrate transportation processes, ordering and manufacturing, order changes, production scheduling, logistics programs, and warehousing operations); Exchange and processing of data between partners (such as exchange and processing of technical information, orders, etc.); Gathering and processing information to analyze the process of sourcing and evaluating, selecting and developing suppliers; Collecting and processing supply and demand information, etc. to predict market trends and future supply and demand conditions; Creating and Improving Relationships Between Partners (Speckman & Miller, 1998, 635).

As it turns out, information management and supply chain information systems can influence many internal decisions of different parts of the supply chain, which indicates the high importance of this component in supply chain management.

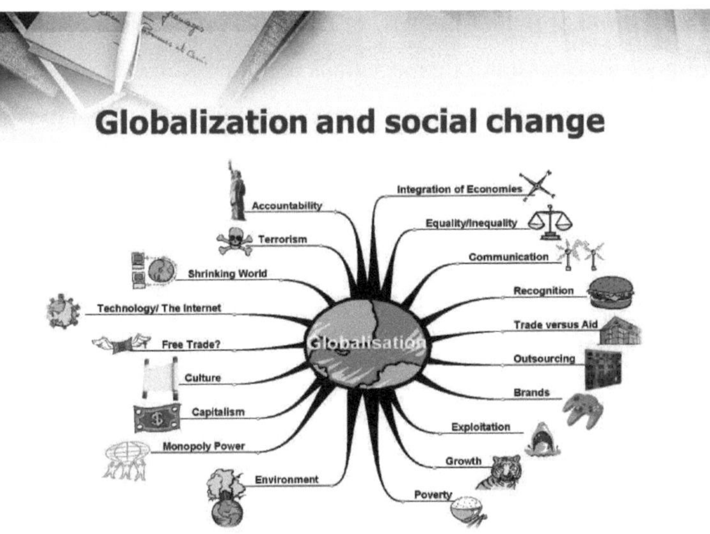

Figure 4. The aspects of Globalization

Logistics management: In the analysis of production systems (such as the automotive industry), the subject of logistics includes the physical part of the supply chain. This section, which includes all physical activities from the stage of preparation of raw material to the final product, including transportation activities, warehousing, production scheduling, etc., occupies a relatively large part of supply chain activities. In fact, the logistics area is not only the flow of materials and goods, but also the axis of supply chain activities, which relationships and information are the supporting tools to improve activities.

Relationship management: The factor that leads us to the end of the discussion and perhaps the most important part of supply chain management because of its construction and form, is the relationship management in the supply chain. Relationship management has a tremendous impact on all areas of the supply chain as well as its level of performance.

In many cases, the information systems and technology required for supply chain management activities are readily available and can be completed and deployed in a relatively short period of time. But many of the initial failures in the supply chain are the result of poor transmission of expectations and the result of behaviors that occur between the parties involved in the supply chain. In addition, the most important factor for successful supply chain management is reliable communication between the partners in the chain, so that the partners have mutual trust in each other's capabilities and operations. In short, in the development of any integrated supply chain, the development of trust and confidence among partners and the design of reliability for them are critical and important elements for success (ibid., 645).

The main phases of supply chain management

Phase I: Conceptual design

The first phase represents the manufacturing strategy. In this phase, how the organization is run is determined by creating an image for the future and creating a structure for implementation. For the first phase processes, a specific organizational model is required that varies from organization to organization. The main discussion in this phase is conceptual design, which is evidence for the validation and implementation of the other two phases. The purpose of this phase is to understand the details of the costs and to identify the system and the benefits of implementing supply chain management.

Phase 2: Detail design and testing

This phase can be performed simultaneously with the first and third phases. That is, details are designed and solutions are tested in the real world at the same time. In this phase, it is recommended to make changes in the structure of the organization and consider them for implementation in the system in order to support the design of the new supply chain.

Phase 3: Implementation

In this phase, following the second phase, the implementation of long periods of operation and changes in the system in order to create facilities is done (Figure 5) (Blington, 1992, 26).

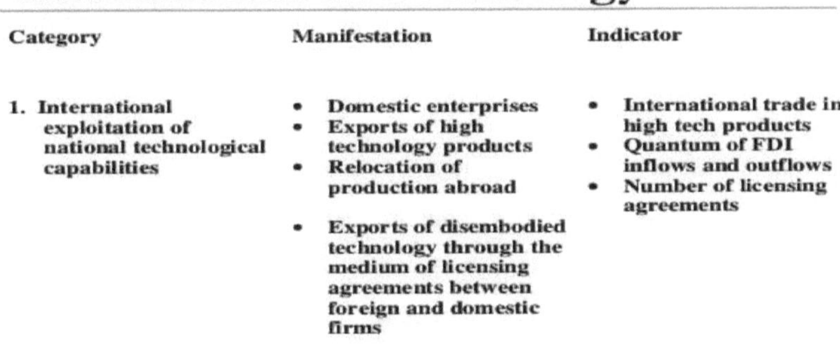

Figure 5. Globalization of technology

Information technology and supply chain management

Supply chain management is based on a customer-centric approach. Accordingly, timely and complete communication between all elements of the chain to know the needs of the customer and the extent of meeting the needs of the chain is essential. To facilitate the flow of information and its accurate management, a suitable platform of integrated software and information systems and extranet and intranet networks are required. By using e-commerce in the supply chain, computer networks, especially the Internet, can be used to describe the operations of buying, selling, and exchanging products, services, and information based on the B2B and B2E models (Heid and John, 1990, 88).

Based on another model of e-commerce, partner companies in a particular field can collaborate and share efforts through electronic networks; Such collaboration often occurs between companies in a supply chain.

In general, supply chain management is one of the e-commerce implementation infrastructures. From an industrial point of view, e-commerce between firms occurs mainly in industries where the supply chain is formed. A producer is always a factor in the middle of the process of economic activity.

The producer is the buyer of the goods from his suppliers and the seller of the new goods to his buyers. Because the seller has suppliers to the producer, and the buyer of the goods may also have customers, we are faced with a chain of firms, each of which is both a buyer and a seller; This set is like a chain, because everyone is interdependent. With proper management of the supply chain, all the elements in the chain benefit and at the same time, by providing high quality and cheap goods, it also benefits the society. Therefore, one of the most important industrial issues in developed countries is supply chain management. One of the important elements of chain management is the automation of sales between members of the chain. This is so important and vital that even before the advent of the Internet, the automotive and aerospace industries, which have the largest and most complex supply chains, had built their own networks at great expense (ibid., 91).

The EDI standard, which is currently used for business purposes in the Internet environment and on the basis of the XML standard for business, with the help of the World Standards Organization, has been created from these dedicated networks. For supply chain management, chain stability is an important and vital factor and usually complex, efficient and stable forms of supply chain management are seen only in large economic enterprises. Currently, there is a serious shortage in this field in our country; On the one hand, the number of large economic enterprises in the country is very small. These small numbers are mostly non-private in nature and therefore face the problem of sustainability in the face of political issues. On the other hand, the number of sustainable supply chains in the country is very small; Two notable examples can be considered the automotive industry and the country's oil industry (Ibid., 95).

Definitions, concepts and topics of customer relationship management, necessity and necessity of implementing customer relationship management

With the transition of the traditional economy and the intensification of competition in new dimensions, the customer as someone who the organization wants to influence his behavior with the values it creates, has become the main pillar and axis of all activities of organizations, in a way Competitiveness, survival and continuity of organizations are expressed in the group of identifying and attracting new customers and retaining existing customers.

On the other hand, the development of communication, the evolution of the information age, and the emergence of new communication tools, organizations with a large number of different customers, has faced them with many choices that result in more customer control and market instability. Management and marketing thinkers have prescribed the version of customer retention and the right ways to communicate with them under the title of customer relationship management, which has been seriously introduced by Tom Sell since 1993 and entered the public sphere. In its simplest terms, customer relationship management is putting the customer at the heart of the business and the highest degree of importance. In our country, although with delays in the global economy, in recent years, customerism issues have opened their place in relations between people with organizations and government relations with people, and the need to pay attention and satisfy the needs and desires of customers in a serious way. It has been felt.

Reasons why organizations move towards customer relationship management

Customer acquisition and retention, customer loyalty and increasing customer profitability are the most important business challenges of today's organizations. Investing in customer relationship management can lead to a variety of benefits. Some organizations are looking to penetrate the market faster and others are looking for greater profitability by lowering costs. But the ultimate goal of all organizations is to develop a strong customer relationship structure and achieve what is needed to maintain a high level of customer satisfaction and loyalty. In the age of online transparency and global choice, organizations can no longer hide behind their policies and prices. Customers are smart enough to know that they have a choice, and if they have a bad experience with the services provided by the organization, they will use this right and go to competitors. In fact, the levers of power have been transferred from the organization to the customers, that is, unlike previous decades when the organization made decisions for customers, now it is the customers who make decisions for the organization (Salehi Sedghiani and Akhavan, 2004, 32).

Research and studies show that the next wave of investment in information technology will belong to customer relationship management, and the trend of applying customer relationship management is expected to grow by 25 to 30% over the next five years. Organizations typically use application software providers to support the integration of their various business functions and hope to invest in customer relationship management to create better customer retention plans and revenue. Increase your permanence. In general, the following reasons can be mentioned for organizations moving towards using customer relationship management. (Dehghanizadeh, Haji Ali Akbari, 2005, 30)

    I. Use current relationships with current customers to maximize revenue growth.

    II. Identify, attract and retain the best customers.

    III. Introduce and identify the most repetitive sales procedures and processes.

    IV. Meet the needs and meet customer demand.

V.   Create and implement an active marketing strategy that leads to cost reduction and deeper customer knowledge.

Traditional marketing experiences in organizations express this in another way: (Dehghanizadeh, Haji Ali Akbari, 2005)

1. The cost of selling goods to a new customer is six times the cost of selling to an old customer.
2. Usually, every dissatisfied customer shares his dissatisfaction with 8 to 10 people.
3. The probability of selling a product to an old customer is about 50%, while the probability of selling the same product to a new customer is only 15%.
4. If the company can increase its annual customer retention by 5%, it can increase its profits by 30 to 125%.

Customer concept

In Persian culture and literature, the concept of "customer" is synonymous with "buyer", and in matters of marketing and sales, the customer refers to an audience that has the ability and talent to buy goods or services. In this definition, "ability" means the ability to pay and "talent" in the sense of understanding and recognizing the benefits of goods and services that meet part of the needs of the audience, is used.

The customer is the one who defines his need, consumes our goods and services and is willing to pay a reasonable price for it. But he incurs this cost when he sees valuable goods and services delivered that justifies the payment. (Khaksazi and Bahramzadeh, 2005, 150)

A customer is a natural or legal person who receives a product or service. Customers are generally divided into two groups: domestic and foreign customers. Foreign customers are divided into two categories: final consumers and middle customers. End consumers use products and services directly, and intermediate customers in the external value chain act as intermediaries between the producer and the end consumer. Internal customers are an organization of employees who receive a product, service, or information in the internal value chain. are. They may be industrial customers (other organizations buy a company's products for use in their operations) or end customers who consume manufactured goods or services directly. Internal customers, on the other hand, are within the organization. They are individuals or groups who depend on other occupations to do their work. Every job or task is both a supplier and a customer. (Guide, 2004, 28)

Customer life cycle

> The term customer life cycle refers to the stages in the relationship between the customer and the business, and awareness of it leads to customer profitability. There are generally four stages in a customer life cycle:

> Potential customers: People who are not yet customers but are targeted by the market.

> Customers who react: Potential or potential customers who respond to a product or service.

> Actual customers: People who are currently using a product or service.

> Ex-customers: These people are not suitable customers because they have not been targeted for a long time or have taken their purchase to competing products. (Shah Samandi, 2005, 82)

Oil and gas companies have always lagged behind the most important digital marketing initiatives and methods

This is of little importance to them because only 7% of the industry's revenue is still allocated to marketing. This trend also applies to the use of new marketing technologies such as automation software, analytics tools, social media and content management. Lack of effort in advertising activities prevents B2B oil and gas companies from being able to withstand a high level of competitive (busy) market. Brands can no longer ignore marketing functions due to the many changes in determining the industry outlook.

The solution lies in investing in online marketing technologies with the approach of increasing the return on equity of shareholders as well as increasing growth. Here are some marketing tips that will help oil and gas companies in this area.

Most companies invest in B₂B online marketing platforms

Many oil and gas activists around the world are realizing the value and importance of digital platforms over time. In addition, according to statistics, 74% of buyers active in B_2B businesses prefer to use an online website to make a purchase (Figure 6).

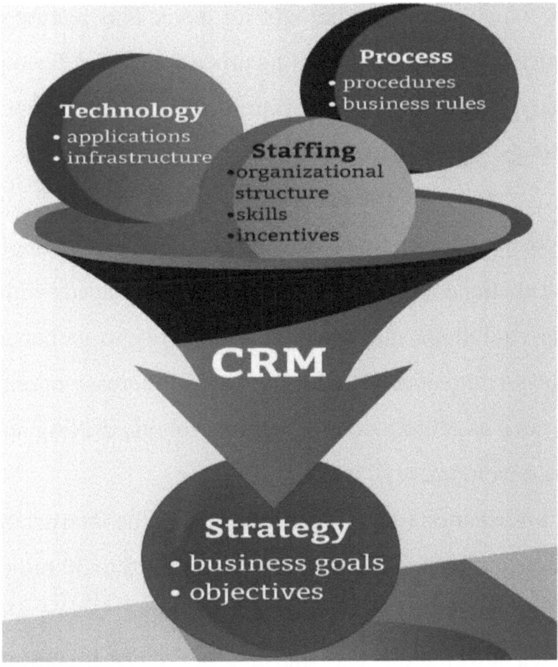

Figure 6. The Definitive Guide to Customer Relationship Management

So, the solution is an online (digital) platform. Digital technology is a common denominator and common denominator of cost reduction, process simplification, productivity improvement and better decision making. Investing in this field is a great guide to building long-term growth and gaining new customers. But many in the oil and gas industry continue to cite the same marketing methods and traditional sales techniques that date back decades. While new online marketing methods provide the ability to integrate and coordinate sales teams, many B_2B businesses, especially in the oil and gas sector, have long cycles for the sales process. The first solution is to invest in an online platform that brings new buyers, service providers and manufacturers together under one banner. Manufacturers and suppliers can create a dedicated page for their company that is a guide to oil and gas topics and where they can showcase their services, products and position and reputation.

Buyers, on the other hand, can visit the platform to get an overview of the different companies and see which one might be right for them. This feature makes it possible to reach a community and make the marketing process easier and companies reach their target audience faster. Technological innovation, artificial intelligence, smart data and the Internet of Things What shapes marketing in the oil and gas industry are the methods that improve practical efficiency.

In particular, equipment vendors are pioneering the use of this technology, which helps customers by using artificial intelligence and meeting their needs with support services such as optimizing equipment maintenance. The ability to gather more information from facilities allows companies to reduce costs and increase operational efficiency. New technologies such as remote-control sensors, robotic drilling and 3D printers are contributing to this development.

A large amount of information (data) is generated using the Internet of Things, and IoT terminals are projected to increase from 13 billion in 2015 to 30 billion in 2020. All of this data is machine-generated data with a very large record and volume. How companies track this information and translate it for use in the marketing process determines their success or failure. Given the benefits of real-time data analytics and the use of IoT applications, companies offer high value propositions to their potential customers, which is a advantage over companies that do not have this option. Utilizing this information by investing in the IoT information system sets these companies apart in competition. They will be able to improve their customers' experiences with better offers and thus increase their satisfaction.

Good interaction with customers through several channels

Today's customers, whether they are regular customers of the Amazon Store or customers of B2B oil and gas business businesses, are eager for a topic and it is a meaningful experience for customers. Now it's time to look at how the marketing channel can make a competitive difference Create one that can help your company stand out in a highly competitive environment. Those who work in the B_2B businesses of the oil and gas industry are those who have just entered the digital space and have accepted it and observed its interesting methods. 98% of all B_2B business customers research online before making a final decision to make a purchase. It is up to the marketer to meet customers wherever they are and to use mobile, laptop, social media, blogs, blogs, etc. To communicate with customers through all communication channels. The goal is to provide as much information as possible to buyers and create a lasting experience for them (Figure 7).

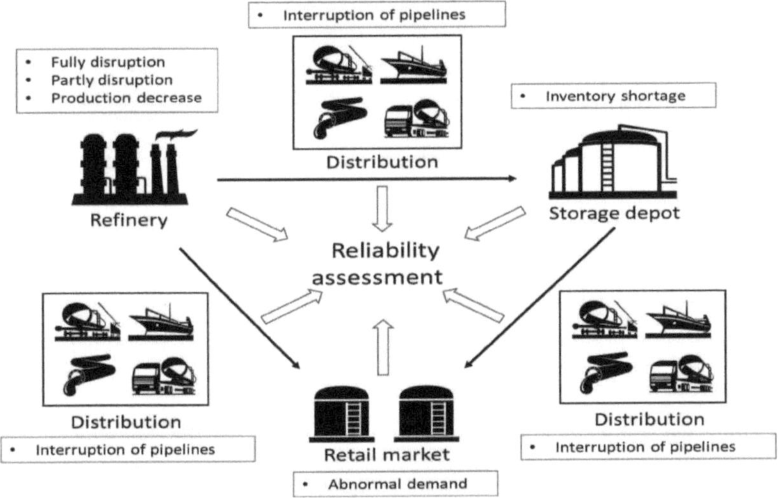

Figure 7. Sustainable refined products supply chain

Good interaction with customers through several channels

Today's customers, whether they are regular customers of the Amazon Store or customers of B2B oil and gas business businesses, are eager for a topic and it is a meaningful experience for customers. Now it's time to look at how the marketing channel can make a competitive difference Create one that can help your company stand out in a highly competitive environment.

Those who work in the B2B businesses of the oil and gas industry are those who have just entered the digital space and have accepted it and observed its interesting methods. 98% of all B_2B business customers research online before making a final decision to make a purchase. It is up to the marketer to meet customers wherever they are and to use mobile, laptop, social media, blogs, blogs, to communicate with customers through all communication channels. The goal is to give buyers as much information as possible and create a lasting experience for them, and it does not matter where they get this information from.

Personalized service Another important way to attract new customers is to provide them with personalized services. This is a progressive and effective process. This is because B_2B companies themselves acknowledge that even personalizing their website has had a huge impact on helping them achieve their goals. They also stated that their customers prefer to buy from companies that offer them personalized services and allow them to shop effortlessly.

One of the B_2B business strategies for oil and gas companies is to show that by investing in dedicated account management, different customer relationships can be integrated and with the help of digital operating systems and communication management solutions. Managed with the customer. Consequently, if marketers want to grasp an important point from what has been said, the point is that it is now essential to embrace online marketing platforms.

To conclude, we refer to the information provided by the McKinsey Institute: Companies that have used the online marketing method have had their revenue growth five times the normal rate. Now this is an issue that is on paper and should be implemented.

In conclusion, CRM can be different in any organization from other organizations. In general, organizations use CRM to capture information, people, and processes Sectors such as sales, marketing and services (dealing with the customer) are interrelated. But the capabilities of each organization to support the workflow and business goals are different from other organizations. Each organization selects metrics to measure CRM success it has the most connection with that organization. Also, the priority of these criteria is determined by each organization and is tailored to its needs. Therefore, merely modeling the criteria of similar or competing organizations may lead the organization to erroneous results (Figure 8).

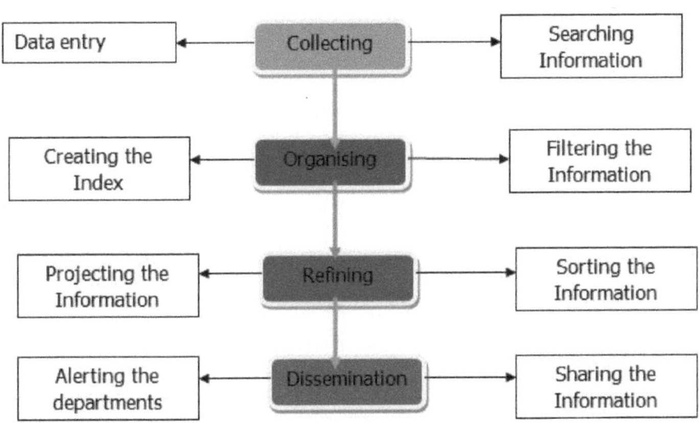

Figure 8. Marketing Management Assignment CRM

Customer relationship trends

The key to business growth lies in its successful relationship with the customer, which includes recognizing and tracking the needs, behaviors and life cycle of the customer and also requires the use of this information to create value for the customer. The most important trends that lead to a value-creating relationship with the customer are: speed of service, self-service, integration, ease of use and customer satisfaction. Trends are global issues that usually start slowly and last for about five to ten years; But as the needs of the organization and consumers increase, they quickly disperse and spread. Now, each of the above-mentioned trends is described: (Dehghanizadeh and Haji Ali Akbari, 2005, 29)

Speed of service: Speed of service to customers is very important. Customers are not interested in delays and are reluctant to wait, and the more time becomes important to them, the more they will look for organizations that provide their services more quickly. As the speed of service delivery increases, customers' expectations for more services increase. Therefore, service utility tools should be easy to use and have a comfortable and friendly atmosphere. Customers avoid slow and difficult business transactions. They usually prefer their service systems, because these systems are active seven days a week and all day and night, and you can search for information and products through these services without the use of sales staff.

Self-Service: Customers' interest and interaction with self-service is great in-service organizations; But before the service itself can become a reality, new infrastructure must be created and new protocols must be designed. In this case, the integration of processes will be necessary. The service itself has caused changes in business processes. When buyers and sellers interact online directly, the role of intermediaries is greatly diminished. Elimination of intermediaries is one of the main features of e-business. The service itself is quite visible in the online aviation and travel industries. In these systems, the customer is able to connect to a central reservation system via the network and act faster and more conveniently to book the flight he wants. This enables organizations to automate the booking process. Self-service reduces costs and eliminates the need for expensive physical equipment.

Providing Integrated Services: Organizations need to use integrated and comprehensive tools that focus on the whole relationship with the customer, instead of focusing on local and superficial solutions that deal only with part of the customer relationship. Have coverage. Integrated solutions and services are one of the essential and vital parts of any business strategy. Consumers have also moved from cross-cutting solutions to integrated solutions. This trend can be seen in many retailers. In these stores, customers want to meet all their needs in one place and under one roof. They need businesses that provide integrated services to meet their one-stop shopping needs and the decision-making process.

Ease of use of services provided: With the emergence of new trends in online shopping behaviors, companies must reduce the processing time between search, selection, ordering and execution in order to be successful. Delays in any of the process steps are not acceptable and at the same time the ease of use of the customer must be fully considered; Because the organization communicates with customers at different levels. Organizations need to share customer service issues with everyone who is in some way in touch with the customer, and instead of sending the customer from one department to another, there is a single point of contact with customers.

Figure 9. Business Background png download - 500*500 - Free Transparent Customer Relationship Management

Customer Satisfaction

A customer is someone who conducts a transaction or trade in a competitive environment and gives and receives something in an interactive mode, and customer satisfaction is an emotional amount that is met by meeting their expectations or adding to their expectations. Gives. Therefore, the customer, the axis of organization and the consumer, is the philosophy of organizations. Therefore, identifying, differentiating, prioritizing, discovering the main expectations and finally obtaining customer satisfaction are among the activities of the organization. The organization must properly understand and consider the issue of audience knowledge, which is one of the basic issues in customer-oriented culture, and update and increase the quality of products and their quantity every year in proportion to increasing customer expectations.

Customer Relationship Management Background

Perhaps the history of the emergence of issues related to customer relationship management can be summarized in the following three periods: (Hypothesis,2007, 27)

The period of the Industrial Revolution: Ford's initiative in using mass production method instead of manual production method, is one of the most important indicators of this period. Although the change in production method reduced the range of customers' choice in terms of product characteristics (compared to handicraft products), but the products produced in the new way had a lower cost price. In other words, in choosing the mass production method by Ford, increasing efficiency and economic efficiency were the most important goals.

Quality Revolution Period: This period began at the same time as the Japanese company's initiative to continuously improve the process. This in turn led to lower cost and higher quality products. This period culminated with the introduction of new methods of quality management such as total quality management. With the increase in the number of companies present in the competitive field and the spread of the culture of maintaining and improving product quality, this competitive advantage was no longer effective for leading companies and the need to find new ways to maintain a competitive advantage was felt.

Customer Revolution Period: In this period, due to increasing customer expectations, manufacturers were required to produce their products with low cost, high quality and high variety; In other words, manufacturers had to shift their focus from production to finding ways to satisfy and retain their former customers. With the widespread use of information technology, organizations can increase awareness of customer needs and better understand them. Benefit from technical knowledge along with the necessary skills. During the 1990s, interactive IT management processes are based on information technology that is at the end of the business process and in relation to the customer. Re-engineered, this issue is now known as "customer relationship management".

Customer relationship management includes all the steps that an organization takes to establish and establish beneficial relationships with the customer and in the form of teamwork to ensure Defined by customer satisfaction. In most cases, such activities are carried out under the title of sales, marketing and specialized services. The driving force behind customer relationship management is the fact that retained customers are more profitable than new customers (Figure 10).

Figure 10. Customer Relationship Management Qualifying Ppt Powerpoint Presentation

The need for customer relationship management

Customer relationship management is a concept that has its roots in sales automation technology and call center operations and has been around since the mid-1990s. At that time, customer relationship management arose from the integration of customer data through the sales department with call center interactions, which led to more informal interactions with the customer. The concept was propagated by user organizations and rapid mergers, prompting software vendors who all claimed to have a coherent set of capabilities known as customer relationship management.

Previously, relationship marketing sought to obtain information about customer preferences stored in databases. This emerged in the form of "one-on-one" marketing, which referred to the process and interactions through companies that created offers that were in line with customer demands.

Therefore, customer relationship management was developed in order to establish security and manage person-to-person relationships and create a beneficial and long-term relationship with customers. In a parallel channel, Internet-based tools such as e-commerce, Internet marketing, and person-to-person communication have evolved and grown. With these new technologies, these products competed outside of customer relationship management and reached e-commerce.

When the concepts of customer relationship management and e-commerce were merged, e-customer relationship management came to the fore in a short period of time. Similarly, the integrated business management system recognized that in a 360-degree view of the customer (ie, a holistic view) they had to consider data transfer, so they developed a complete software package with customer relationship management capabilities. From a technological point of view, customer relationship management includes a set of applications that address the wants and needs of customer-facing roles, leading to the feeding of a shared database supported by business analytics tools. (Osranko and Banani 143, 2007)

CRM software is used in many marketing activities such as market segmentation, customer acquisition, customer retention and expansion. Operational CRM, however, includes service and sales functions. Developing CRM software to support an organization's mission to become more customer-centric often means a wider distribution of customer data throughout the company, not just in marketing. Operations management can use customer data to produce personalized goods and services.

The human resource management department can use customer data on the products they prefer to attract and train staff who are in direct contact with the customer. Research and development management can use customer data to focus on new product development. Customer data is not only used to integrate the company's internal departments, but can also be shared among external companies, including suppliers and partners.

The third misconception: CRM is an issue in the field of information technology (IT) Due to the need to store, analyze and report large volumes of data among different departments as well as partners of the organization in a short time; There is no doubt that IT is required to create CRM in many companies. CRM technology is advancing and can be costly; So it is very easy for senior management to use IT to lead CRM. CRM technology provides a tool to create more value for the customer and the company. The two main parts of most CRM projects are people and processes. People develop and apply IT-created practices.

IT cannot be a good tool for some incompatible processes and people. CRM application will be considered successful when it involves people who design and implement value-added processes for the customer and the company. Most of these processes are done in the IT context; So, IT is part of most CRM strategies. Keep in mind that not all CRM applications will include IT. The main goal of many CRM projects is to develop and maintain relationships with valuable customers. This may be accomplished through behavioral changes in store employees, training of staff who are in direct contact with the customer, or a focus on improving sales force skills, and IT has no role in any of these projects.

Customer loyalty schemes are commonplace in many industries, such as car rental, the airline industry, hotels, and food retailers. Customers receive credit for the purchases they make, and these credits will later be converted back into money. Most loyalty schemes require new members to fill out a form as they enter the program. This census-related information is often used in conjunction with purchase data to make customer relationships more efficient and product development more efficient. Although some

CRM applications are in line with customer loyalty plans, not all of them are used for this purpose.

Loyalty schemes play two roles in CRM application. First, they generate data that can be used in the process of attracting, retaining, and developing customers. Second, loyalty schemes can also be used as a barrier to exit, as customers who have gained a lot of credibility may be reluctant to disconnect.

The accumulated credit indicates the value of the customer's investment in the loyalty plan and consequently in the relationship between the company and the customer.

Strategic CRM can be implemented in any company. Every organization wants to be more customer oriented. Senior executives can create a vision, mission, or values that bring the customer to the heart of the business. CRM technology may play a role in this transition, and some companies are definitely more successful than others. The banking industry uses CRM extensively, however there is a big difference in the level of customer satisfaction and retention of different banks. Any company can try to implement operational CRM.

Any company with sales force can automate sales, customer management and communication management processes. The same is true for marketing and service processes. CRM technology can also be used to support marketing campaigns, support requests and complaint management. Analytical CRM has a different theme from strategic and operational CRM and is based on customer information and data. This information is at least needed to identify which customers will generate the most value in the future and to divide customer databases into segments tailored to customer needs; Then, various offers are offered to each group of customers in order to optimize the value created for the customer and the company in the long run. If this data is lost, analytical CRM implementation will be impossible

Customer relationship management goals

The goals of customer relationship management can be listed as follows:

- ✓ Increase revenue.
- ✓ Recognize new business opportunities.

✓ Reduce missed opportunities.

✓ Reduce customer flight.

✓ Build customer loyalty.

✓ Improve customer service.

✓ Improve the appearance of the organization.

✓ Reduce costs.

✓ Save organization information.

✓ Reduction of marketing rework (Niknia, 2007, 53).

Objectives of customer relationship management from the perspective of thinkers

Objectives of customer relationship management from Barnett's perspective

Barnett states that the goals of customer relationship management can generally be divided into three groups: cost savings, revenue growth, and strategic impact. (Figure 11) (Barnett 2001, 42).

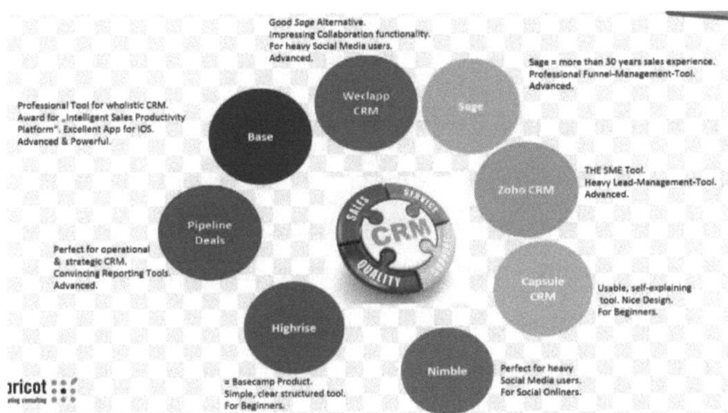

Figure 11. Marketing Background png download - 1782*1082 - Free Transparent Customer Relationship Management

Increase sales revenue: When organizations spend less time collecting customer information, they can pay more attention to their customers, which is effective in increasing their revenue.

Improving Success Rate: Organizations avoid customer mistreatment in the sales process by implementing customer relationship management.

Increase profits: as a result of recognizing customers, offering value and discounting prices to them.

Different generations of CRM

This section describes the various developments that have taken place in CRM since the 1990s.

First generation (functional CRM)

The set of activities, later referred to as CRM, was initially presented as two independent products. "Sales force automation" and "customer support and service". The purpose of automation of sales force and support and initial service was to improve service and sales; But it could not do well, and instead the market for enterprise resource planning was growing.

Second generation (Integrated Customer-facing Front-end)

During this period (1996), the innovations created in CRM during the 1990s were adapted to the innovations in ERP, and the independent subsystems became integrated. In addition to emphasizing sales and customer service performance, marketing performance was also discussed during this period.

The goal of CRM in its second generation was to reduce the cost of customer engagement, increase customer retention, and enhance the customer experience of the product.

Third generation (strategic approach)

In late 2002, the CRM market began to grow, narrowing the gap between customer perceived value and customer value. Organizations learned from their experience and failures in using previous versions of CRM. During this period, the evolution of Internet technology contributed to the rapid development of CRM. Many organizations have found that they can benefit from adopting a strategic CRM approach instead of blindly using technological solutions. During this period, organizations realized that the ultimate goal of CRM is not only cost control, but also revenue growth.

Fourth generation (agile and flexible strategic CRM)

In the late first decade of the 21st century, the fourth generation of CRM began. During this period, strategic CRM was widely adopted and used as a core component of marketing strategy, and an increasing number of small and medium-sized companies adopted this management tool and its coordinating technologies to move their business. Agility, flexibility and low fixed costs were the solution. The advent of social media, the rise of self-service, and the proliferation of web-based services all meant that delegating authority to the customer were new issues that organizations needed to address.

One-to-one customer risk management in financial and credit institutions

When small and large financial institutions face the challenges of the worst economic crisis (since the Great Depression), they can take a risk-taking approach to retail credit card customers by influencing their success in overcoming the current storm and building beneficial relationships. Give the customer a try and enjoy the benefits. By applying the best practices and the most advanced one-to-one customer risk management analytical tools throughout the credit cycle, organizations can minimize deficiencies in current collections and maximize retaining beneficial customers for long-term growth. The credit card debt crisis that Business Week described as its "future analysis" on October 9, 2008 did not arise overnight and will not disappear slowly or quickly. This is a sign of bigger economic issues, often created by the philosophy of "more credit for all", which, of course, was prevalent in the previous decade.

Excessive correction management This model shows that even with the current approach to risk management, the financial institution is significantly weaker after 6 months. Lack of passive retention and absorption activity in an area where customers are fleeing to large and scattered financial institutions leads to a significant decline in the collection. Obvious inactivity is practically a negative action that has a long-term impact on the company. The six-month results for the overhaul approach are even worse than issues such as existing responses to the credit crunch. In the beginning, over-correction is apparently better than not taking any action, but after 3 months, it is costly to continuously make a quick profit and reduce the risk of wholesale. Brand cohesion, customer trust, and strategic risk management that lead to growth are non-existent, and this model represents a whole new set of issues that can increase the depth and duration of an institution's recession. These additional issues affect most customers who are already losing out on their financing, lack of trust in financial institutions, and consequently risk.

Eliminating customer credit, lowering interest rates, or incurring higher costs will almost certainly jeopardize current and future relationships with those customers. In this model, the lack of other lines of trade (DDA, deposit accounts, mortgages, etc.) of customers dissatisfied with their behavior as credit card holders is not reflected. But a very clear and obvious risk is reflected. Each of these factors leads to what may seem like an unexpected conclusion at first. An increase in rates and costs, called risk management, is likely to lead to a practical reduction in interest income, costs, and turnover. Such actions leave good customers behind while they can gain credit elsewhere.

Jevelin's research and strategy make it clear that "there is a war going on for deposits. "The ability of banks and credit unions to strengthen their deposits continues in the direction of which one survives when the banking crisis deepens and which one fails." Failure to take advantage of opportunities to attract new customers, especially profitable customers, who move away from their banks, complicates matters. As the recession spreads, eliminating unprofitable customers without attracting profitable customers will lead to more revenue cuts. Compared to the above over-correction problems, the 1: 1 CRM approach significantly reduces the risk of alienating good customers with short-term risk reduction strategies that should focus only on weak risks. This process leads to the refinement of the selective set and the support of the improved targeting of new and quality customers.

1: 1 CRM enables firms to maintain valuable customer relationships during the current crisis as an inflexible basis for high and future sales and growth opportunities.

Implement 1: 1

CRM principles So how can a financial institution launch 1: 1 CRM?

The following three conventional principles guide the successful 1: 1 CRM implementation process and address key challenges in marketing analysis across financial institutions. First, banks need to adjust their existing marketing models to better reflect current risk tolerance. They also need to adopt new analytics tools to help identify behavioral goals for predicting when existing customers will be at greater risk, which may result in their deactivation, which in turn may require an incentive to restart or increase cost allocation. To be. Success in the first stage requires better penetration of behavioral information, transaction data and payment data.

The next step for a successful 1: 1 CRM focuses on the strategy management process. According to a 2008 Aite Group survey (Marketing Analysis Trends in Retail Financial Services) by 24 retail financial services companies, database marketing strategies are hampered by inflexibility:

> ➢ Sixty-three percent of respondents believe that the process of designing and implementing new models is fragmented or challenged.
>
> ➢ 62% of respondents claim that the model development cycle is always very long.
>
> ➢ 59% of respondents report that they are never or rarely able to implement quick and correct scenarios of the relevant strategies.

Tools and techniques are available to facilitate faster data aggregation, strategy design, model creation, and strategy implementation.

Process modification should leverage cross-sectional channel information and bridge the gap between marketing and risk management. The third key step is to implement a successful 1: 1 CRM focus to effectively guide the strategy through the fit of the modified proposal. This scenario is based on a better understanding of the habits of separate credit card holders and the maximization of efficient communication channels.

1: 1 CRM to attract credit card holder

As reflected in this model, maintaining the first stage of the credit life cycle during times of crisis is critical. Continuous "good customer" recruitment efforts are necessary to maintain profitable customer accounts and begin the collection cleanup process. Financial institution marketers are severely confused by direct response rate values, which have fallen from an approximate level of 1.4 percent in 1995 to 0.6 percent in 2008, which is affected by the saturation of influence and growing post volume.

To implement a 1: 1

CRM throughout the acquisition process, banks can begin by better shaping the principles of the current risk set within their target marketing. In other words, they do not spend money on applications that do not seek correction. Current absorption models need to be modified to focus less on simple reaction or response values and more on good customer response or response. A return to fundamentals approach should focus on changing the targeting of the strategy.

Principle-based strategy tools can assess the ability of future cardholders, stability and willingness to pay. Such tools should see credibility well beyond the office privileges. These core benefits are useful for identifying eligible and non-eligible applicants, but a significant portion of potential potential customers are in a "gray area" above or below the average cut-off or reduction score. Card issuers can maximize the effectiveness of their marketing investment through the use of tools that better evaluate those "gray area" customers by analyzing more accurate data such as geography, demographics, mortgage status, medical payments, job changes, Changing the address and date of writing the check, as well as other key information that can make a customer more or less risky.

For example, individual reviews of applicants with previous bankruptcies should confirm that not all bankruptcies are the same. Nearly one million Americans go bankrupt for two years because of medical expenses. They have the ability and inclination to repay standard debts other than hundreds of thousands of dollars in medical bills. Market segment bankruptcy treatment in a model based on the principles of attraction can enable credit card issuers to accept old and useful customers. Modified targeting is the first step to successfully implementing a 1: 1 CRM for uptake.

But as all marketers know, the success of this strategy lies in delivering the right offer to the right customer at the right time. In November 2008, Aite Group surveyed 100 U.S. credit card issuers (titled Overcoming Credit Card Challenges), rewarding respondents as the most important single variable in attracting Loyality cardholders, along with custom product production, distribution channels, and tolls. They considered the price low. The growth of reward-sponsored reward schemes enables banks to have a significant opportunity to differentiate their schemes and focus on rewards based on individual cardholder habits, while reducing the costs associated with rewarding cash or increasing the value of customer rewards.

Acquiring skills in a broad channel strategy is important for card issuers whose recruitment models are fully dependent on direct mail. With customers flocking to larger banks and all financial institutions, those who can make the most of the leverage of multi-product / multi-channel customer communications win.

For the recruitment strategy, this means more effort in offering cross-cutting rewards, targeting and focusing on DDA customers by resorting to card offers and using branch, internet banking, ATM and reciprocal (IVR) domains to deliver cross-selling messages.

1: 1 CRM for account maintenance

In Phase 2 of the Credit Cycle, Account Maintenance, and Default, the 1: 1 CRM re-evaluates the health of the institution's credit card and manages a two-pronged approach on an innovative basis. On the one hand, systems need to be in a position to tightly monitor credit risk and examine customers who are either troublesome or at risk. On the other hand, in order to maximize the value of the existing collection, card issuers must actively convert inactive accounts and keep customers at risk of expanding and directing growing activity among loyal customers.

Behavioral modeling, access to traditional data sources such as credit history and demographics, as well as less obsolete data such as spending patterns and payment dates, can lead to significant improvements in risk assessment and the ability to predict volatility. It can also not be valuable in targeting and focusing on offers that go directly to specific customers (based on purchase date). Aite Group's survey of marketing analytics found that only a handful of financial institutions currently use behavioral data in their account and non-collection processes. However, most expect the cost allocation for this type of information to increase over the next 3 years.

When retaining scarce marketing resources in the face of pressure to reduce customer erosion, a regional bank determines which customers to target and which on-demand marketing offer to be appropriate and efficient. For this purpose, a predictive model for structuring was provided to the bank.

Analyzing historical transaction data over a 2-year period for 2 million accounts resulted in erosion points being transferred to each current credit card holder. The survey found that one percent of specific customers deactivate or cancel their account within the next 60 days. This analysis provides erosion scores for each cardholder and provides valuable information that can be used to design effective strategies to retain customers with the highest erosion risk.

For example, the results showed that customers with the least use of their cards in gas pumps are more likely to cancel their accounts. This is an unexpected finding that enables the bank to Target diesel advertising strategies. The bank uses customer-centric advertising strategies for those accounts that are likely to close within the next 60 days.

The highest focus is on the 10% of customers who are most likely to erode. By dividing them into several categories based on demographic habits and cost allocation and spending trends.

Targeting the most at-risk customers allows the bank to focus on its resources and where they are most focused. Separation of these customers has allowed the bank to design effective marketing measures to increase card usage and reduce the likelihood of erosion. Preliminary results indicate that this approach was a success. Banks are expected to increase their credit card usage by up to 8% (along with a 6% drop in erosion).

Finally, automated communication tools are available for efficient and temporary management of cost-effective credit risk. Phone calls, personal voice messages, emails and SMS are useful for activating the account and advise customers to use the cards and remind them of overdue payment habits. Loan payers can review existing accounts (active and inactive) and start contacting customers to update demographic information and determine the overall health of the loan.

If cardholders file bankruptcy or financial statements, some accounts require risk management, interest rate control, and fee reduction. When risk management techniques are combined with customer service features, overdue debt rates are as low as 20% in high-risk collections, and customers are able to repay their loan and thus remain in a good position. The combination of automation and personal loan review demonstrates the power of 1: 1 CRM in strengthening a set of financial institutions.

1: 1 CRM for collection sets

Receipts (the third stage of the credit cycle) still present another unexpected situation in this economy. In theory, most current levels of consumer debt should result in a myriad of transactions, whether creditor or in the form of debt collection institutions and buyers. In practice, however, lower liquidity results in lower collection success, resulting in higher global costs per dollar collected. This puts increasing pressure on collection agents to better target their strategies. Receipt operations pay considerable attention to predictive analytics and automation tools such as decision engines and automated dealers and software delivery via WEB or IVR technology to correct receipt success rates and prioritize activity. There are even more problems or problems in certain sectors of the industry, such as card issuers. Customers consistently report credit card issuance as the lowest priority when clearing their monthly debt.

The results of a case study show that a large financial institution will be able to adjust its annual revenue to $ 1.2 million with this solution, which will enable the institution to accelerate its adoption of liquidation bids by as much as 90 days in arrears. These old tools can help you focus on the main accounts. All ATMs have a kind of "rule engine" that uses "If-Then" logic to distribute accounts through the workflow process. The better the engine of principles and regulations, the more efficient and effective this process is.

The number one obstacle to the successful application of the "engine of principles" enhancement tools is the lack of internal IT resources to make changes to a time-consuming model. Efforts have been made to reduce the complexity of this engine of principles and to facilitate the activities of the internal operations teams of the institutions to work on the systems. Traditional analysis solutions are consistently more accurate than predicting human behavior. However, they are effectively integrated with other tools for cost-effective evaluations of potential actions, so existing scores still need to be reviewed through the principles engine to complete the decision. What is missing, of course, is a decision engine, at least until recently.

It is a software tool that a typical operations manager or business analyst can use to combine the most advanced predictive analytics with business analysis tools and the principles engine. Of course, a human being is still needed to implement the strategy and set the company's global goals, which directly evaluates each individual account, which are: The accuracy of predictive analyzes increases through the reduction of human error Productivity is enhanced by evaluating more accounts The goal of an automation decision engine is to make most of the decisions in an account in a way that significantly simplifies the principles engine in downstream systems.

Chapter III

Increase customer satisfaction

Reduce administrative marketing costs and general sales costs: When organizations become specialized and have good information about their target customers; This is true and they make better use of their resources and no effort is wasted on them.

Objectives of customer relationship management from a zero point of view

Knoll stated that the key to customer relationship management is identifying the things that create value for customers, then delivering them. In this view, while customers have different attitudes to value, there are many ways to satisfy each of them. (Knoll, 2000, 11). Therefore, the goals of customer relationship management are:

- ✓ Identify the specific values of each segment of customers.
- ✓ Understand the relative importance of those needs for each customer segment.
- ✓ Determine whether presenting such values in a positive way will be effective.
- ✓ Communicate and present the appropriate values to each customer in the way they want to receive information.
- ✓ Measuring results and proving return on investment.

Customer relationship management goals from Swift's point of view

Swift stated that the goal of customer relationship management is to increase business opportunities through the following.

- ✓ Improve the process of communicating with real customers.
- ✓ Provide the right products to each customer.
- ✓ Provide the right products through the right channels to each customer.
- ✓ Provide the right products at the right time to each customer.

By doing so, organizations gained the following benefits:

- ✓ Customer retention: The ability to retain loyal and profitable customers and channels for business profitability growth.
- ✓ Customer acquisition: Acquisition of real customers based on their characteristics that cause growth and increase profit margins.
- ✓ Customer profitability: increase the profit margin of each customer while providing the right products at the right time.

Objectives of customer relationship management from the perspective of Galbraith and Rogers (Figure 12).

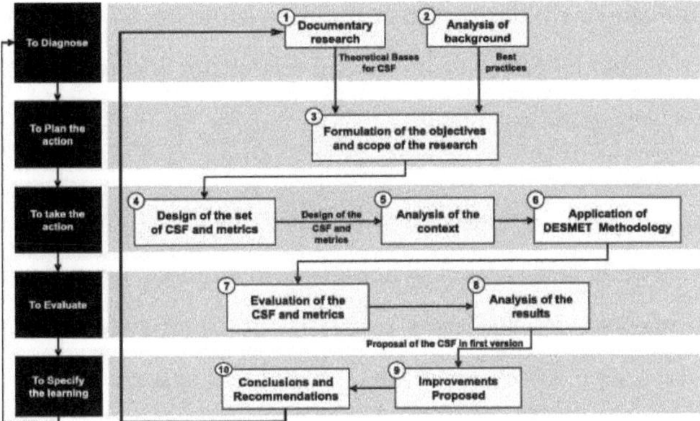

Figure 12. Critical success factors for a customer relationship management strategy

These two researchers believe that many factors influence the customer's purchasing decision. Customers buy products and services that meet or exceed their expectations and capture the attention of employees.

An organization is required to meet customer expectations in a consistent manner to help its long-term survival. This issue has a special validity today despite the cruel and global competition. They consider the three main goals of customer relationship management to be customization, personalized communication, and after-sales support services. (Galbraith and Rogers, 1999, 48)

Customization: Customers want services that meet or exceed their needs. Providing such services and products is a necessary activity for the line and growth of the business. The key to the success of organizations lies in guiding the specific and unique characteristics of each customer. This is called mass customization, which is economical in scale while seeking to produce products that meet the needs and wants of each customer.

Personalized Communication: The biggest correlation with success is the amount of time spent by the customer, leading to two-way personal communication and trust. Creating a relationship with the customer requires suppliers to pay closer attention to customers. This means listening to them, actively using feedback that will improve these communications and their results.

After-Sales Support: Paying attention to the after-sales customer by providing active and responsive services and support, when many customers, after experiencing after-sales service / support, try to leave suppliers. It can have many effects on the profitability of the organization. Therefore, one of the ways to ensure customer loyalty is not to forget them, even after the products are consumed.

Customer Relationship Management Objectives from the Perspective of Calcutta and Robinson

According to these researchers, customer relationship management is a kind of integrated framework and business strategy. They have identified three goals for the customer relationship management organizational framework:

- ✓ Use existing customer relationships to increase revenue (increase profitability by identifying, attracting and retaining the best customers). This is done by providing a comprehensive attitude towards customers to maximize their relationship with the organization through sales (sales of exclusive products) and sales of ancillary products (sales of complementary products).
- ✓ Use integrated information for superior services (use customer information to provide better services). By doing so; The organization creates customer time savings and customer-specific information should be available to all contact points.
- ✓ Introducing processes and methods that are consistent with the individual or customer contact channels, more employees are involved in selling products and services. In order to have a consistent position, organizations must have consistent and comfortable interactions with customers everywhere.

Explain the different definitional dimensions and features of customer relationship management

Customer relationship management, sometimes referred to as customer management, customer value management, customer-centric or customer-centric management, has long been a common term for companies' desire to communicate one-on-one with one another.

In this regard, it can be acknowledged that companies that have succeeded in effectively attracting their customers, providing them with the desired services in the best way and retaining their best customers will have a positive impact. At the end of the road, they have seen their profitability. With the advent of e-commerce and new economic conditions, the development of stronger relationships with customers has become more important. Customer relationship management is a strategy in which a stable and long-term relationship is established with customers, tailored to their circumstances and patterns of behavior, which creates added value for both parties. Customer relationship management strategy is usually based on four executive goals, which are:

> Encourage customers of other companies or potential customers to make the first purchase from the company.

> Encourage customers who have made the first purchase to make subsequent purchases.

> Convert temporary customers to loyal customers.

> Provide high service or utility to loyal customers in a way that becomes the company's value.

In fact, customer relationship management is all the processes and technologies that the organization uses to identify, select, persuade, expand, retain and serve the customer. Customer relationship management will enable managers to use customer knowledge to increase sales, service and development, and increase the profitability of ongoing relationships. Customer relationship management is based on the exchange of value between the customer and the organization and emphasizes the value created in this relationship.

Therefore, the efforts of organizations to develop long-term relationships with customers, based on creating value for both parties are one of the main goals of customer relationship management. In other words, the goal of customer relationship management is to provide benefits through mutual exchange and fulfillment of promises. Customer relationship management is a business strategy that is enhanced by the advancement of technology and through it, companies create useful communications based on optimizing the received and perceived value of customers. (Niknia, 2007, p. 53) (Figure 13).

Figure 13. Customer Relationship Management Growth Ppt Powerpoint Presentation

The characteristics of customer relationship management are as follows: (Mahdavi Nia and Ghodratpour, 2005, p. 22)

1) Collecting and consolidating customer information, which includes the following:

  ✓ Use of proprietary software to analyze this information.

  ✓ Market segmentation based on the value of life expectancy of the customer.

  ✓ Micro-segmentation of the market based on the needs and desires of customers.

2) Calculate the long-term value of the customer.

3) Customer segmentation based on their value (profitability) and prioritization between departments.

Principles of customer relationship management

Customer relationship management processes and applications are based on the following: (Gary Webbon, 2001, 1)

Targeting individual customers: One of the principles of customer relationship management is that customers have many choices and each customer demands its own products and services. Customer relationship management treats each customer individually as it is based on a philosophy of customization and customization. Customization means that the themes and services provided to the customer should be designed based on their preferences and behaviors. This will make the customer more comfortable and increase the cost of changing the seller.

Attract and maintain customer loyalty through personal communication: When customization takes place, organizations need to maintain that relationship. Continuous customer contact - especially when these calls are designed to meet preferences - can lead to loyalty.

Customer selection based on the concept of customer lifetime value: In customer relationship management, the principle has been considered that different customers have different value for the organization, so the most profitable of them should be attracted and retained. Through differentiation, an organization can allocate its limited resources to achieve better returns. In short, product customization, customer loyalty, and their selection based on the concept of lifetime value are the basic principles of implementing customer relationship management.

The main elements of customer relationship management

The content of the customer relationship management strategy includes six interrelated indicators proposed by Othello and Donaldson in 2002, which are:

1) Emphasis on quality - Poor service is the main reason for business failure. The product alone is not enough and the quality of service is the key to the success of a business.

2) Measuring customer satisfaction and managing customer service - This refers to understanding and identifying the various benefits that exist for a customer before purchasing. The gap between expectations and performance after the purchase process must also be managed.

3) Investing in Employees - Internal relationships are just as important as external relationships. The implementation of relationalism can only be achieved by people in the organization who understand the goals and standards set.

4) Maintaining customer dialogue - building long-term relationships is a key issue in customer relationship management. Companies that listen to the preferences of individual customers are more likely to retain and convert them into loyal customers.

5) Set realistic goals and achievable actions - Organizations should understand as much as possible how customers perceive and perceive the various elements offered to them.

6) Relationship-Based Encounters - This means that both groups of domestic and foreign customers are available to behave in a flexible and responsive manner. In practice, there is always a gap between what the company does and what it should do and the most desirable thing to do. With the help of relationalism, it is possible to adapt to the needs of each customer. (Osranko and Banani, 16,2007)

Basic assumptions of customer relationship management

Habit-based actions

The basic idea of customer relationship management is that the future behavior of the customer is determined by their similar or previous behavior. In other words, people behave like yesterday or the month before. This assumption is partly true and partly false. Behavior patterns change over time. The important thing, then, is to anticipate future behavior so that the organization can better serve the changing demands and preferences of its customers (Figure 14).

Figure 14. Excellent Examples of Customer Relationship Management (CRM)

Current customer information is always correct.

Maintaining the quality of behavioral and demographic information of customers (age, gender, income, etc.) is very important. The right decision requires the right data and information. Can we trust and believe the data in databases or data warehouses? Customer databases are obtained from different sources and by different input methods. It is necessary to pay attention to sorting and clearing data periodically and for a considerable cost to be useful for use in customer relationship management. Institutions should be updated as soon as customer information changes. For example, they move, their income levels change, marriages, births, and deaths occur, and although many of the right decisions are sometimes made from the wrong data, they rarely happen.

Successful customer relationship management requires a large, centralized database with complete customer data.

Many successful financial-level companies maintain some kind of database. With a small database, organizations can simplify system and customer design and maintenance. Adherence to standard hardware and software standards is more important than having a large database. (Elahi and Heydari, 2005, 23)

Customer Relationship Management Lifecycle Model

In his model, Kalakota considers customer relationship management to consist of three stages of attracting, promoting and retaining, each of which supports recognizing and understanding the relationship between the organization and its customers.

These steps include:

- ✓ Attracting new customers; By promoting the leadership of goods and services.
- ✓ Promoting profitability of existing customers.
- ✓ Maintaining profitable customers for their life; By focusing on transforming the services that customers want, not the market.

This theory states that each stage affects the relationship with customers in different ways in such a way that the strategies and focus of the organization are different from each stage to another. This is shown in the table below. (Table 1)

Table 1. Stages of customer relationship management and their respective attention and organizational strategies (Johnson and Storm, 2002, 1)

strategies	The focus of the organization	the level
Innovation	Differentiation	Absorption
Reduce customer service costs	cluster	Upgrade
Listen to the customer offering new products	Conformity	Preservation

Customer relationship management process

Kai Tom sees customer relationship management as a process that revolves around transforming customer information and knowledge into interaction and then communication with them. This process involves several important components (Kai Tom, 2002, 1):

- ✓ Insight (derived from) the customer
- ✓ Value obtained by the customer
- ✓ Marketing planning
- ✓ Customer interaction
- ✓ Analysis and refinement

Customer Insight

In order to maximize customer satisfaction, revenue and profitability, the necessary insight should be obtained from them by analyzing customer information. This continuous learning also includes acquiring product information, market distribution routes and competition. Market opportunities and strategies are identified and developed through this type of customer knowledge exploration.

Customer value stage

Includes actions to identify the most valuable and loyal customers and then change the goods and services to suit them. Loyal customers provide higher return on investment over time.

Marketing planning stage

Includes conclusions from the knowledge gained. At this stage, strategic communication plans are developed. This step defines customer offers, routes, types of competition, scheduling, and more.

Customer interaction

It is an important practical step that separates the created plans from the previous stages, ie customer insight and marketing planning. The main goal of this step is to maximize the compatibility of all points of customer interaction with all routes. This step involves implementing and managing communications using a range of routes and applications such as call and customer care applications, interactive applications, and sales applications.

Analysis and refinement

It is a kind of learning process that is obtained by collecting and analyzing information resulting from interaction with the customer. By performing analyzes, insights are obtained from customer information and can be used to improve communications, prices, approaches and all aspects of strategic planning.

Customer needs

Customer needs Due to the presence or absence of the relevant feature, causes a situation in the customer. It is divided into three categories:

basic needs : There is a need that if it is not in the product, it will not be accepted by the customer and will cause objection and non-purchase by the customer. (Bashiri,2001, 47)

Functional needs: If this need is not met, it causes customer dissatisfaction and may choose the desired product, but if it is met, it also leads to customer satisfaction and satisfaction (Bashiri, 2001, 47)

Attractive need: A need that is met will lead to customer satisfaction and over-satisfaction. In connection with this need, it should be said that if it is not present in the product, it will not cause customer dissatisfaction. It is also argued that needs become one over time, and that an attractive need may become a basic need over time. For example, in the last few decades, having a radio recorder in a car has been an attractive need, but now it has become a basic need that, if not met, will lead to customer protest. (Bashiri, 2001, 94)

Executive Challenges of Customer Relationship Management

- ✓ The main challenges that an organization may face in implementing customer relationship management can be divided into the following three main cases: (Dehghanizadeh and Haji Ali Akbari, 2005, 29)

A. Initial start-up cost - Initial start-up cost is one of the challenges of customer relationship management. Organizations may have invested heavily in customer management tools. Because some of these tools may have specific applications, they can hardly be shared in different sections.

B. Integrated application tools - Organizations need integrated application tools based on customer life cycles and customer interactions. Organizations that need to manage customer interactions in different languages and currencies will not be able to manage customer relationships through outdated technologies, and this will be very difficult for them.

C. Collaboration of different sectors - Customer relationship management is an integrated approach and requires the cooperation of parts of the business that have previously operated independently. Data collected in one section must be shared in all other sections. Some departments may be reluctant to share their data with others (Figure 15).

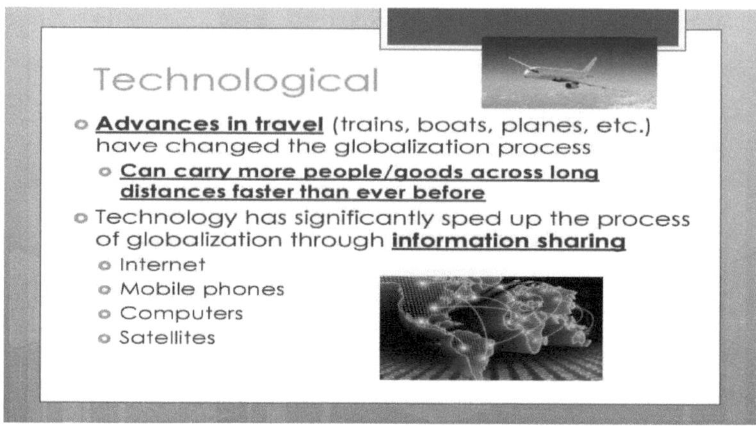

Figure 15. Globalization

Steps of implementing customer relationship management

To implement any project, you must first research its advantages and disadvantages. It should be noted that the benefits of this project outweigh the costs. For this purpose, in the implementation of the customer relationship management project, seven steps are briefly described: (Mahdavi Nia and Ghodratpour, 2005, 23).

Step 1) Hardware and Software Benefits Analysis - The benefits expected from the project must first be identified. Customer relationship management considers three important financial benefits, which include increased revenue, reduced costs, and increased customer satisfaction. The first two are the hardware benefits of customer relationship management, which are easier to measure than its software benefits, such as customer satisfaction.

Step 2) Cost Evaluation - To start customer relationship management, you need to make an investment to buy technology, including hardware and software, and need a network. Numerous studies, however, have shown that the cost of such equipment is only a small percentage of the total cost of manpower and the cost of processing variables. To ensure that all costs are taken into account, both manpower and processing costs must be included in the purchase price of the new technology. Finally, the costs incurred for the new technology must be offset by the costs incurred.

Step 3) Real-time framework - If the implementation of customer relationship management is timed, the expected benefits of implementing this method can be evaluated by implementing this method in a specific period. Cost savings and revenue increases occur before there is an improvement in customer satisfaction.

Step 4) Unchanged scenario - that is, what will happen if nothing changes. Current net income and customer satisfaction should be compared with current costs and predicting cost improvements or increased costs.

Step 5) Determine the return on your customer relationship management project implementation - As with all forecasts, this is not an easy task. Forecasting is intertwined with problems such as measuring software benefits, especially those related to customer satisfaction. To facilitate such problems, measures can be considered, which include:
- ✓ Assistance from sales, marketing and services in the evaluation work.
- ✓ Develop a range of estimates and estimates to reduce forecast risk.
- ✓ Talk to industry experts and peers about the rate of return they are earning or expecting to earn.

Step 6) Compare Estimated Returns with Existing Resolution - Once the returns are determined in the current context and after the implementation of customer relationship management, the two should be compared. If the implementation of customer relationship management provides an increasing return, the customer relationship management project should be implemented.

Step 7) Ensuring Returns - The key to the success of a customer relationship management project is the commitment of the organization's top management to the project. In addition, the key factor requires a leader and an experienced team to manage the project. Implementing a customer relationship management project, like all projects done in a company, must have a good return. Therefore, great care must be taken in the implementation of this project. Because with the wrong choice, opportunities and as a result, a lot of profit may be lost.

Incentives to pay attention to customer relationship management

Internal stimuli of the organization

Increasing attention to customer relationship management is due to some specific stimuli, each of which can lead to a new approach in this area.

- ✓ **Pareto Law:** This law recognizes that 20% of an organization's customers generate 80% profitability.
- ✓ In the field of industrial goods, selling to a new customer requires 8-10 physical calls, but selling a product to an existing customer requires 2-3 calls.
- ✓ Attracting a new customer is 10-5 times more expensive than repeating existing customer transactions. Biston Consulting Group, for example, has shown that the cost of marketing existing clients via the web is $ 6.80 compared to attracting new clients via the web.
- ✓ A dissatisfied customer shares his experiences with 8-10 other people.
- ✓ A 5% increase in customer retention costs translates into a 25% or even greater increase in profitability.
- ✓ In the past, the primary approach to customer retention was mainly to use postal and media advertisements for what institutions were offering. But this advertising approach is massive and targets many people (including current customers and people who never become customers). (Gary and Bowen, 2001, 10) (Figure 16).

Customer Relationship Management ERP

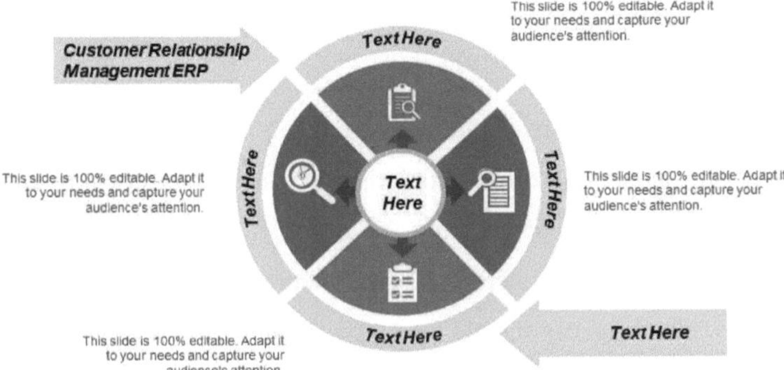

Figure 16. Customer Relationship Management Erp Ppt Powerpoint Presentation

Stimulus for e-commerce

Changes in e-commerce are another factor in the move toward customer relationship management. They take action. Therefore, organizations do not need sales skills to convince the customer.

Stimulus costs targets

- ✓ Increase revenue growth in terms of increasing customer satisfaction (for example, by increasing sales of by-products or repeat purchases).
- ✓ Reduce sales and distribution costs (for example, by increasing the likelihood of product acceptance by advertising tools, use the web to reduce the number of vendors and distribution channels needed).
- ✓ Minimize customer support costs (for example, by making customer information available to resellers, automating call centers for direct reseller access to customer preferences and purchase history).

Types of customer relationship management technologies

From a technology perspective, customer relationship management includes a set of applications that address the wants and needs of the customer and lead to the sharing of a shared database supported by business analytics tools. (Osranko and Benini, 24, 2007). The technologies used in customer relationship management can be divided into three general categories, each of which can be implemented separately. (Hypothesis, 2007, 28)

Operational customer relationship management

In this method, all stages of customer relationship, from marketing and sales to after-sales service and receiving feedback from the customer, are entrusted to one person. One of the tools and methods of operational customer relationship management is sales force automation, which is responsible for all operations related to call management, stock exchange and sales department management. Customer support systems are another tool of customer relationship management, an operation in which instead of telephone communication with the customer, other tools such as face-to-face communication, Internet, fax and customer response kiosks are used. Also in this case, the company prepares itself for its responsibility to the customer and a company's internal systems are placed in this section. For example, all parts of a company such as services, ordering, billing and marketing are included in this section, and the only thing that should be considered is the coordination of the systems of this section with the current systems in the company.

Operational Customer Relationship Management Supports traditional transactional processes that take place in the form of systems with operations performed in the front office and on a daily basis in order to communicate directly with customers. Operational customer relationship management has the role of supporting the strategic analysis and back operations of the organization. The primary difference between operational and analytical customer relationship management lies in the type of direct relationship between the organization and its customers. Table (2) shows the different technologies of sales, marketing and customer service that are used in the implementation of customer relationship management operations, the description of each of which is as follows (Baltzan and Phillips, 2008,283).

Table 2. Operational customer relationship management technologies

Marketing	Sale	customer services
List Builder	Sales Management	Call center
Activity management	Call management	Web-based self-service
During sales and after sales	Opportunity management	Write down conversations

Marketing and operational customer relationship management

Companies are no longer trying to sell a product to as many customers as possible, but they are trying to sell as many products as possible to one customer. The marketing department has the ability to collect and analyze customer information with the help of customer relationship management technologies. (Baltzan and Phillips, 2008, 184).

List Builder: List creators collect customer information from a variety of sources and segment it based on different marketing deals. Sources of information include website visitors, website questionnaires, online and offline questions for current customer lists, and more. After compiling the customer list, the organization can filter and group its potential customers according to its criteria.

Activity Management: Activity management systems guide users through in-house marketing that includes definition, design, planning, segmentation, and analysis. These advanced systems even have the ability to quantitatively calculate the results of the rate of return for each activity and use the results to analyze and understand how future activities will work.

In-sales and after-sales: Two important strategies that develop marketing activities are in-sales and after-sales strategies. In-sales strategy means selling additional services or products to a customer. McDonald's, for example, does its after-sales service by asking customers to request larger meals. Customer relationship management systems provide all kinds of customer information to marketing departments. In this way, it helps them to identify their marketing activities during and after the sale (Figure 17).

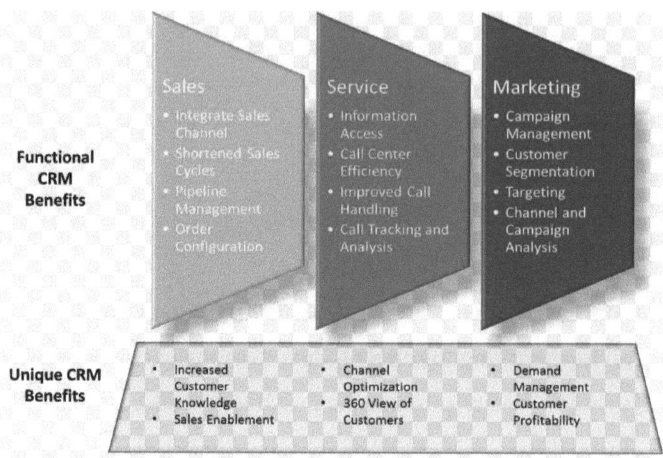

Figure 17. Brochure Background png download - 900*604 - Free Transparent Customer Relationship Management

Sales and operational customer relationship management

Sales departments were the first place in the organization to start developing customer relationship management systems. These sections had two main reasons for tracking sales information to customers electronically. The first reason was that agents and resellers had difficult conditions with huge amounts of customer account information and wanted to maintain and classify them.

The second reason why companies were so involved was that much of their sales and customer information was only available to their sales agents. One of the key components of customer relationship management that helped solve this problem was sales force automation. . Sales force automation A system that automatically tracks all stages of the sales process. Products pay a lot of attention to increasing customer satisfaction, building customer relationships and improving product sales by tracking all sales information. The three main customer relationship management technologies that the sales department can use to satisfy customers are: (Baltzan and Phillips, 2008, 286).

a. Sales management systems Customer relationship management.

b. Call management systems Customer relationship management.

c. Customer Relationship Management Opportunity Management Systems.

Sales management systems Customer relationship management

Potential customers are like blood for the life of organizations. Sales Management Systems Customer relationship management mechanizes each step of the sales process, aids in personal sales, and coordinates and organizes their accounts. Features include scheduling customer appointments, reminders and alerts for important tasks, and document creation. Even these systems have the ability to analyze the sales cycle and examine how each person performs during the sales process.

Customer Relationship Management Call Management Systems: Customer Relationship Management contact management systems record and maintain customer contact information and identify and identify prospective customers for organizational charts, additional sales information, and detailed customer notes. For example, a call management system can take incoming phone numbers and display the caller's name along with notes and details from previous conversations (Figure 18).

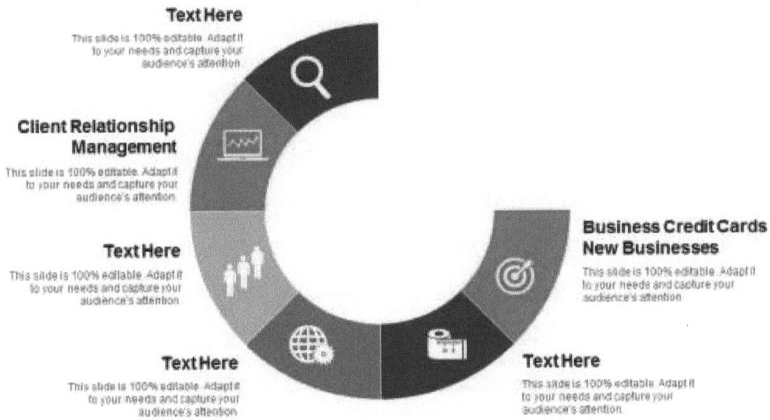

Figure 18. Client Relationship Management Business Credit Cards New Businesses

Customer Relationship Management Opportunity Management Systems:
Customer Relationship Management Opportunity Management Systems address sales opportunities by finding new customers or companies for future sales. Opportunity management systems identify potential customers and competitors and define sales efforts, including budgets and plans. Advanced opportunity management systems can even calculate the probability of a sale and are also able to store sales representatives and the cost of each of them in order to find new customers. The main difference between opportunity management and call management is that call management is related to existing customers while opportunity management is related to new customers.

Customer service and operational customer relationship management

Sales and marketing are the major areas that are in direct contact with customers before sales. Many companies have realized the importance of building strong relationships through marketing and sales efforts. Furthermore, they have found that many failures are due to a lack of attention to the importance of continuing the after-sales relationship. Therefore, it is very important that the relationship continues after the sale. Because this issue is essential to ensure customer loyalty and satisfaction. The best way to implement after-sales customer relationship management strategies is through customer service.

One of the main reasons that a company loses its customers is that customers have bad experiences of the company's services. Providing superior customer service is a difficult task, and many customer relationship management technologies are able to help the organization accomplish this important activity. The three main operational customer relationship management strategies in the customer service sector can be implemented to increase customer satisfaction, which are:

a. Call center

b. Web-based self-service

c. Writing conversations

Call center (call center)

Where customer service providers; Respond to customer requests and respond to customer problems through contact points. A call center is one of the best valuable assets a customer-centric organization can have. Because having a high level of customer support is very important and vital in attracting and retaining customers. There are now many systems that enable the organization to mechanize its call center systems, including voice response exchange systems, predictive dialing and automatic call distribution system. Call centers also call Track customers along with their problem solutions, so that they provide crucial information to create a comprehensive view of a particular customer for the customer service representative. The customer service provider can gain a full understanding of a customer's products and problems and provide great value to him or her and the organization.

Web-based self-service: Web-based self-service systems allow customers to find answers to their questions using the Internet. Another feature of the web-based self-service system is the click-talk buttons. Click Buttons - Talk allows customers to call an online service provider 7 at the click of a button. Such important features cause the organization to create great value for itself by providing timely information to customers and without direct customer contact with company representatives.

Writing Conversations: Being a customer service representative is not an easy task, especially when the company's product is technically complex. Writing systems have access to the organization's databases, which identify questions with similar themes and automatically provide details to customer service providers to get those answers to the customer. Even this system is able to create a list of questions so that the sales representative can ask them to the customer and identify potential problems and solutions. This feature helps customer service providers to answer difficult questions quickly (Figure 19).

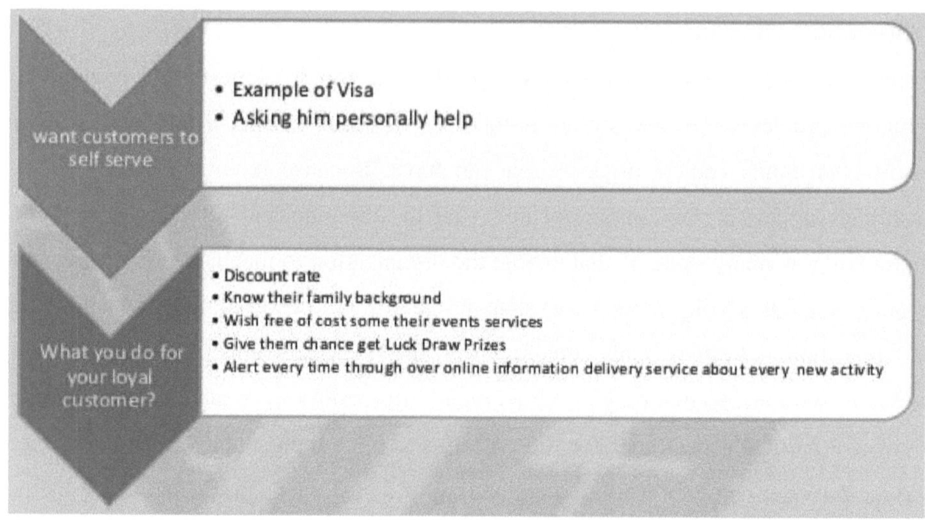

Figure 19. TCS (Customer Relationship Management)

Analytical customer relationship management

In analytical customer relationship management, tools and methods are used that analyze the information obtained from operational customer relationship management and prepare the results for business performance management. In fact, operational and analytical customer relationship management are in a two-way interaction, that is, the data of the operational department is provided to the analytical department; After analyzing the data, the results will have a direct impact on the operational sector. With the help of the analysis done in this section, customers are categorized and it is possible for the organization to focus on a specific section of customers and the data that programs need to communicate with the customer is obtained, ie data Raw materials are provided to customer relationship management programs, and after working on this data, the appropriate result is provided to the company and the customer. In general, it can be said that customer relationship management is analytical, obtaining, storing, processing, interpreting and reporting to users of customer data. (Hypothesis, 2007, p. 28).

The maturity of analytical customer relationship management technology and behavioral modeling technology has helped many organizations to fulfill their main mission of increasing customer service and maintaining a system that truly leads to the right way. To increase the profitability of the business. Unlike customer relationship management, operations that mechanize call centers and sales forces lead to increased customer interaction, analytical customer relationship management solutions are designed to conduct in-depth searches for historical customer information and behavioral patterns.

Analytical customer relationship management is used to support decision making, which accomplishes this task by identifying patterns and by collecting customer data from various operational customer relationship management systems, and for many organizations, The power of analytical customer relationship management solutions creates many management opportunities. Depending on a particular solution, analytical customer relationship management tools analyze customer information and present it in formats such as customer value, product similarity, segmentation, percentiles, and cost. Personalization occurs when a website can detect people's interests and reluctances.

Many organizations now use customer relationship management to create customer rules and patterns so that marketers can personalize customer messages. The information generated by analytical customer relationship management solutions can help companies make decisions about how to create value for each customer. Analytical customer relationship management can provide information about clients that should be highly invested, clients that should be moderately invested, or clients that should not be invested at all.

Customer data can also be given to employees. Analytical customer relationship management relies heavily on data storage technologies and business intelligence to provide insight into customer behavior. These systems rapidly distribute customer information through the organization collecting, analyzing, and distributing. (Baltzan and Phillips, 2008, 28)

Interactive customer relationship management

This part is the point of communication with the customer and it does not have to be how to communicate with the customer; Email, fax, telephone, website, letter, face to face communication or other methods. Interactive customer relationship management Due to the possibility of choosing the method by the customer and the fact that most processes (from data collection to processing and referral of the customer), in the shortest possible time reaches the relevant manager, causing the customer to return and continue communication with Participates.

The use of advanced information technologies enables multiple channels to communicate between the organization and customers. These channels create opportunities for the organization to interact and collaborate with its customers. Systems including interactive channels with customers are known as contact points. This part of the customer relationship management structure reflects how the organization adapts to its customers through business practices that lead to building and strengthening customer relationships.

Proposed models for implementing customer relationship management

Presented in the literature review for implementing customer relationship management. The first model is the Wiener base model.

Wiener model

    A. **Creating a customer database:** The first and most important step to manage customer relations is to create and have a database and customer information. *The database should contain the following information:*

    ✓ *Transactions:* should include complete purchase history and details.

    ✓ *Customer contacts:* includes all customer contact points.

    ✓ *Descriptive information:* This information is used for segmentation and other purposes of data analysis.

    ✓ *Response to stimulus marketing:* includes whether the customer has reacted to direct marketing, sales contacts, etc. or not.

    ✓ Permanently required data (Figure 20).

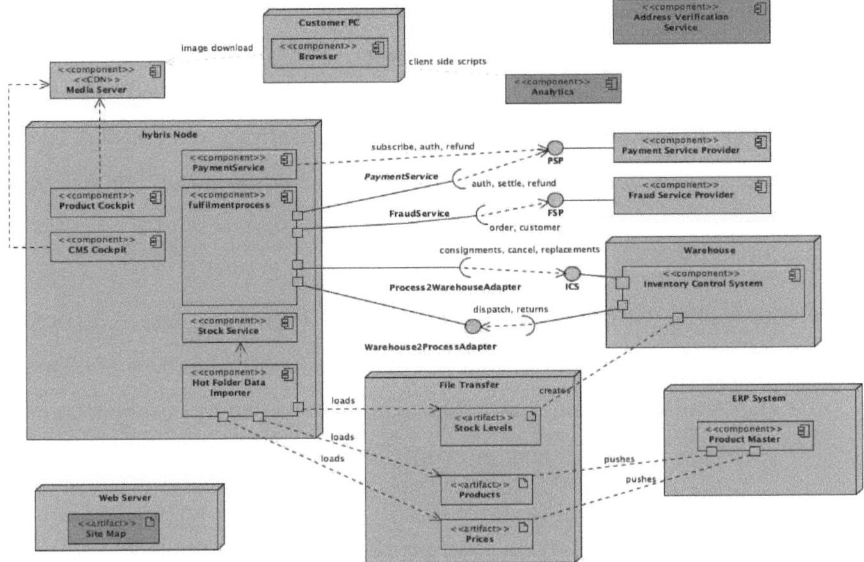

Figure 20. System Architecture of SAP Commerce Accelerator

B. **Data analysis:** The customer database is analyzed with the intention of identifying customer groups. Different statistical classification methods are used to group customers with the same behavioral patterns and data. A new kind of analysis created by the Internet. Click flow analysis is based on mouse clicks on viewing and online shopping.

C. **Customer selection:** After analyzing customer data, the next step is customer selection to target customer relationship management. The results of the analysis can be of different types. If the type of classification is based on purchase, customers in the upper class will be selected first. Customers are usually selected with more profitability.

D. **Customer targeting:** The traditional method for targeting selected customers is direct marketing, but the new one-on-one marketing method through the Internet establishes a relationship with the customer.

E. **Customer Relationship Program:** There is a strong relationship between customer satisfaction and profitability. Figure 2-7 shows the communication program.

F. **Private topics:** With the studies conducted by Forrester 3 research company, the following chain of confidential information concerns has been obtained:
   - ✓ Discomfort and annoyance that are mainly caused by unsolicited emails.
   - ✓ Feelings of abuse and insecurity due to the availability of personal information.
   - ✓ Concern about injury and that people did not want others to know about them.

Companies have come to the conclusion that obtaining information from individuals should not be done in secret, and thus the following two choices were considered in obtaining confidential information:
   - ✓ **OPT-IN:** In this case, web users agree to collect and use their personal data.
   - ✓ **OPT-OUT:** According to this view, the customer should explicitly prohibit the collection and use of his personal information in case of dissatisfaction.

G. **Measurement:** Some of the items that are the basis of measurement in customer relationship management are mentioned below:
   - ✓ The cost of acquiring a customer
   - ✓ Rates of change from viewer to customer
   - ✓ Maintenance rates
   - ✓ Sales rates to some customers
   - ✓ Loyalty measures
   - ✓ Customer participation

All of these measures are to increase customer satisfaction and focus.

SAP accelerator model

Usually, large companies providing software packages also offer implementation methodologies due to the implementation of customer relationship management in different companies. SAP Company has also provided the ASAP methodology, which is a well-known and valid method. SAP Accelerator Methodology is a proven, reproducible and successful method for implementing SAP solution in industries and customer environments. ASAP has phases of project preparation, business plan, research, final preparation, implementation and support, which are mentioned in the continuation of continuous improvement.

Project modeling

Project preparation: The main purpose of this stage is to prepare the initial plan and initial preparation of the project. Training the project team and ordering the initial hardware is one of the main activities of this phase. At the end of the project, the project is at a high level and the project team is organized.

Business work plan: The result of the business work plan is the detailed documents that are collected from the items of demand and need of the organization. Identify business processes and form checklists, interface reports, conversions and increments are the output of this phase.

Realization: The purpose of this step is to implement all business processes based on the business work plan. Unit testing, integrity testing, development, clearing, final readiness, data collection, evaluation and testing, and training of process owners are among the activities of this phase. The key output is end-user acceptance (Figure 21).

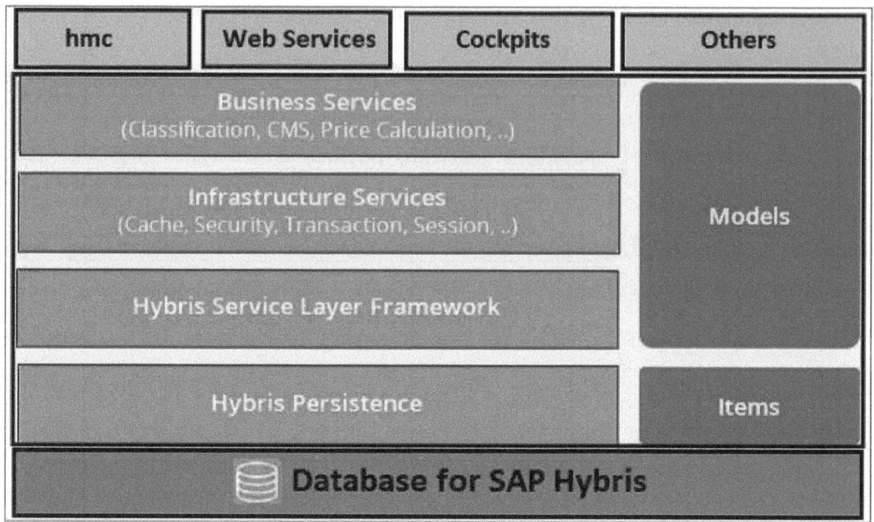

Figure 21. Accelerators Concept

Final preparation: To get ready (including testing, end-user training, system management and final shear activities) to perform in this step. Successful completion of this phase prepares the company to implement the SAP system. This phase includes the final audit of the system, training of end users, general cutting and readiness of support.

Implementation and support: After the completion of the above time, the entire SAP system is implemented in the organization, which includes the activities of reviewing the idea, reviewing the processes of the system and continuous improvement.

Customer relationship management framework based on the type of customer information

In the early stages, the firm identifies the customer by recording customer-related information. Customer registration in membership programs is one of the ways to identify customers. Then the company can provide information related to the organization, its products and services to its customers using bulletins, emails, etc.

After a period of satisfactory relationships, a number of customers become the company's main customers and the firm enters the development phase in customer relationship management.

At this stage, the main customers are actively interacting with the company and the company's customer-oriented foundations are developed through word-of-mouth marketing. Feedback or suggestions received from key customers are also used to introduce new products, improve organizational processes and meet customer needs. At this stage, the barriers between the firm and customers are reduced as much as possible (Park and Kim, 2003, 146).

Model of customer relationship management blocks

Given that the business objectives of implementing customer relationship management include the following, this model is based. Ensure that both the company and the customer have a simple view of each other.

- ✓ Constant customer downturns are maintained and used in customer service.
- ✓ Personalized interaction with the customer is established.
- ✓ Customers are obtained through channels dedicated to their needs.
- ✓ Provides database management equipment for business-to-business analytics.
- ✓ In this development, customer relationship management is based on four blocks: mission statement, processes, customer information and technology.

In this approach, the mission statement of the customer relationship management system is issued by the CEO to the whole organization, IT processes, domestic and foreign trade with integrated customer-oriented approach, customer information into three main categories, customer data, business interactions and the history of interaction is stored in the customer database that can be analyzed according to customer needs (Theo, 2000) and empowerment technology is the other three blocks.

Customer Relationship Management Model - Irish

The Irish Customer Relationship Management model was first implemented in the Irish Group. The results of the project are derived from various concepts of customer relationship management system such as strategy determination, customer-centric business process reengineering, human resource management, computer system and improvement management, summarized in the following sections. (Chalmat, 2005, 37) (Figure 22).

✓ Prerequisites and project management

✓ Determining the organizational framework of the organization

✓ Determining the customer strategy system

✓ Designing a customer relationship evaluation system

✓ Process map

✓ Management and organization of human resources

✓ Creating an information system

✓ Execution

✓ Monitoring

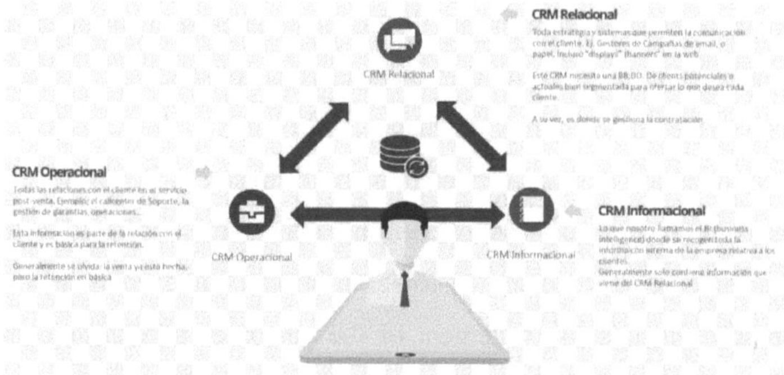

Figure 22. Free Transparent Customer Relationship

Prerequisites and project management: All steps should be managed and monitored in the same way and as an engineering project (Chalmata and Granj, 2005, 121). Project management should be done with the techniques and methodology used in the engineering project and with the forms, evaluation, management and monitoring:

✓ *Before starting the project:* increase management awareness, determine the assigned goals and the overall goal of what will happen in the end, form a team, determine job positions for participation, develop and approve the project plan and internal distribution.

✓ *When the project is done:* implement control and monitoring of time errors, prevent change resistance, employee motivation, measure the degree of participation and evaluate the results.

Organization framework: The starting point of customer relationship management is the analysis of goals and culture (policies and values). The fact that the organization is work-ready and the financial results are satisfactory does not mean that the goals are fully identified. Before starting a customer relationship management project, knowing the organization's strategy, determining where the organization is, where it wants to go, and where it is really going is as important as analyzing the organization's culture and levels and internal controls.

Customer strategy: Creating an effective system for relationship management, the organization needs to change the behavior and know the customer relationship management strategy. For this, the organization should:

a. *Knowing the customer:* The customer should be known and his behavior that can influence should be considered.

b. *Customer profitability analysis:* includes the following tasks:

✓ Organizing customer types into different sections based on variables obtained such as revenue.

✓ Allocation of costs to different departments based on customer-centric cost model (customer relationship management costs) which includes cost characteristics for customer relationship management.

✓ Analyze customer value of revenue, profit and profitability.

c. *Identifying customer goals:* includes the simulated income and expenses of each customer and the goals of each customer.

Customer Relationship Evaluation System: Customer satisfaction is important for the company's competitive advantage and customer acquisition. To improve it, it is necessary to recognize the customer's needs, expectations, and ensure that they are met. This requires the structure of a metering system fed by information that is extracted directly from the customer and part of the company's computer system. The method of obtaining and using this information must be specified. To design a customer relationship management index system, the following is done:

- ✓ Recognize the assigned measurement scale.
- ✓ Error prevention by recognizing the quality dimension.
- ✓ Having the right weight for the scale.
- ✓ Comparison with competitors.
- ✓ Measure non-customers.

Process map: This stage is similar to a re-engineering project that involves redesigning the marketing processes of the customer-centric company to achieve predetermined goals and develop customer satisfaction and loyalty. To create a process map, it is necessary to:

I. Analyze the current situation (from-is) with questionnaires and interviews with employees, and

II. Design the organization's customer relationship management processes that should be (to-be) in the future at the level of detail and depth of models. In order to achieve improvement in customer-related processes, it is necessary to have a basic model with the best example. Models should be public and valuable to any organization. General models are not very detailed and are usually limited to re-engineering customer relationship management processes and are a guide to better goals. In this model, first, information is collected through questionnaires and interviews in customer relationship management support processes, and then based on model information, the details of the work performed in customer relationship management event processes are performed.

Human resources: People are the key to customer relationship management strategy. They are the cause of success and failure and they should not be considered worthless. They need to know the value of the customer and learn the philosophy of customer service. It is essential to create a culture of partnership with a well-known customer-centric approach that enjoys collaboration between management and employees. In addition to changing the culture, the customer relationship management project also requires the new structuring of jobs and the organization diagram in the form of customer teams that are employees of different departments such as marketing, design and sales.

Computer system: To properly implement the customer relationship management strategy, technology is needed to automate and improve the allocation of business processes by managing the company's customer relationship in marketing, sales and sales services. All activities performed with the customer must be stored in the activity database.

This history enables the employees of the organization to know the customer in a timely manner and at any time and his demands that have been met, and provides personalized services. In the automated customer relationship management system, updated records of all activities with the customer, including executions, purchases, requests, complaints, reports and in general direct and indirect contacts with the company are recorded and maintained. IT solutions are combined with learning customer information from the organization and using technologies to manage activities and turn them into business knowledge. (Chalmata and Granj, 2005, 134)

Data mining, statistical analysis, and computer system design of customer relationship management is an artificial technological integration that allows communication between the front of the organization (sales, marketing and customer service) with the organization behind the scenes (financial, Logistics, warehousing, accounting, human resources, etc.). (Stars and Forrest, 27, 2002) (Figure 23).

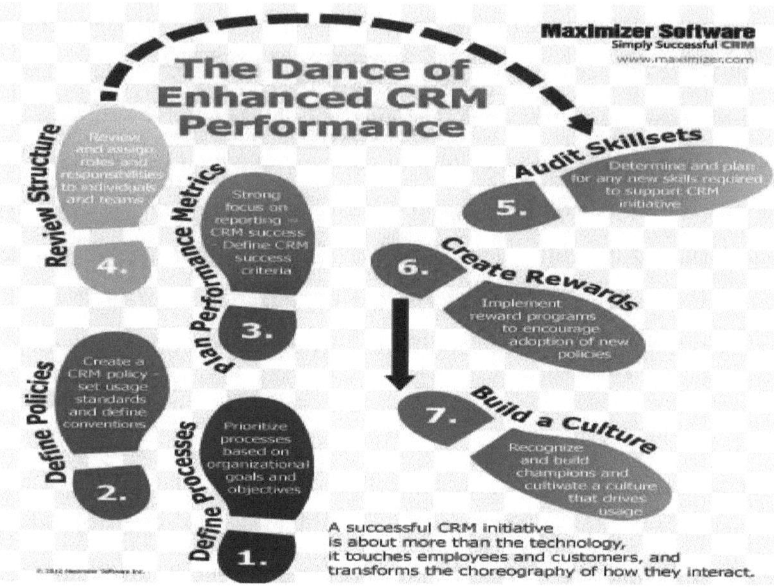

Figure 23. Free Transparent Customer Relationship Management

Customer call management is achieved through communication channels and allows the flow in the system with regular organization and using data analysis tools. Figure 3-8 shows the four main areas of the customer relationship management technology model with the following components:

- ✓ *Interactive customer relationship management (operational):* including marketing (call management, sales management, customer positioning teams, customer observation and interaction, activities), sales (aggregated with orders, billing channels, etc.) and after sales (Reports, complaints, etc.).

- ✓ *Analytical customer relationship management:* includes the integration of the data collection process, turning it into information that is important for identifying customer relationship management and determining project improvement, which helps to draw an integrated customer relationship improvement plan.

- ✓ *Strategic customer relationship management:* directly measures customer profit and short, medium and long goals Determines the duration. (Kerry, 27, 2000)

By this part of the organization Ability:

- ✓ Categorize your customers into different sections.
- ✓ Analyze customer value based on cost model.
- ✓ Calculates revenue, profit and profitability of each customer and each customer segment.
- ✓ Effectiveness.

Customer Relationship Management: Enables company and customer employees to access the information of all customers, retrieve sales and after-sales at the right time with Internet and web services, business portal. Customer relationship management simplifies the call and enables the customer to solve their problems with online questions.

Implementation: The next step is the model of comprehensive quality plan and implementation and control of migration from the old system to the new system. The new plan should be broken down into a set of projects taking into account the financial and physical capacity of the organization. To do this, improvement projects are replaced with projects (from-is, to-be). Then the method of doing work in management and staff is specified and the open organization diagram is re-engineered. To increase the chances of a position it is necessary to:

Develop a partnership plan that includes identifying the exact purpose of the project and then partnering to achieve:

- ✓ Integrity of all members of the organization.
- ✓ Determine the starting point and the end point at any time.
- ✓ Gaining knowledge of how goals are achieved and awareness of the resources that are consumed.

Creating work teams: To manage change, it is necessary to form work teams that are responsible for the changes and transfer them to the organization and the activities of the organization.

Finally, a master improvement system should be created that:

1- Allows future implementation of long-term and medium-term improvement projects.

2- The company accepts changes in the environment.

Monitoring: During project implementation, a team monitors the indicators identified in the initial project management phase and avoids the activity from the ineffective outcome that may occur. The control tool performs this monitoring. In this control, different types of successful indicators are used to monitor each activity.

So far, a lot of research has been done on supply chain management and customer relationship management, and some of the internal research done so far will be mentioned here.

A research entitled: Presenting a multi-criteria decision model to select the best suppliers in the supply chain by combining the process of hierarchical analysis and ideal planning (a case study of the automotive industry) was conducted by Gholam Hossein Soleimani Shiri in 2009. In this research, the relationship between product characteristics and supply chain strategy has been investigated and the level of performance criteria of a supply chain operational reference model has been used as a decision criterion. Also, multi-criteria decision-making methods based on the process of hierarchical analysis and ideal planning have been used to consider quantitative and qualitative factors in supplier selection.

Also, in 2009 by Mohammad Reza Tabibi, Nader Mazloumi presented an article entitled: "Presenting a model for analysis, selection and implementation of business supply chain strategy." In this paper, this scientific management structure is explained by two prominent and major features of supply chain and strategic management under the title of strategic supply chain management from the traditional structure. For this purpose, the components of the strategic management model and the relationships between them from the perspective of the statistical community, ie managers of agricultural businesses operating in the Tehran Agricultural Commodity Exchange, have been identified, screened and analyzed by structural equation method. Based on the results, it is clear that although managers pay attention to most of the identified and explained variables of strategic management, but they are not aware of the relationship between them and how to use it. Finally, the strategic management model presented in this article will be their solution.

A study entitled "Presenting a method for measuring supply chain agility using a combination of graph theory, matrix approach and fuzzy logic" was conducted by Ahmad Jafarnejad, Ali Mohagheghr, Maryam Darvish, Mehrdad Yasai in 2010. In this article, the authors first address the importance and necessity of production chain agility. In their view, for the ever-changing environment of this era, supply chain agility is a vital factor that affects the competitiveness of organizations. In order to create an agile supply chain, it is first necessary to clarify the meaning of agile supply chain, because agility is a very broad concept and has different dimensions that cover different aspects of the organization. In general, although much research has been done on agility, the concept of supply chain agility has not been much explored. Such a situation indicates the need for a technique to measure supply chain agility. The purpose of this paper is to present a technique for measuring supply chain agility, which combines graph theory and matrix approach with fuzzy logic and conceptual structured modeling. This technique has been used in a case study and the main barriers to supply chain agility have been identified in this case study.

In 2005, an article entitled: "Supply Chain Management and Information Technology Support" was presented by Alireza Pouya. According to the author, for proper supply chain management, we need to ensure excellent customer service, low costs and short cycle times. There are several types of supply chains, the most important of which are "integrated fabrication for storage", "continuous filling after unloading", "custom-made fabrication" and "channel assembly". Supply chain management is difficult despite the uncertainty in supply and demand and the need for coordination between several partners' business activities. The main problems are "leather whip effect" and "deceptive storage". There are solutions to supply chain problems, including "vertical integration", "appropriate inventory", "environmental uncertainty reduction strategies" and the use of "appropriate planning and production techniques and techniques". Information technology has also taken an effective step in solving these problems by supporting the proposed solutions. The second form of IT supply assistance is through the e-commerce function, which is provided by automating processes and integrating core business activities through an electronic structure. But order execution in e-commerce is also very difficult for customers due to the need to carry small packages of goods, which can be solved through solutions such as same-day delivery and even the same time and automatic warehouses.

In 2004, an article entitled: "Supply Chains" was presented and compiled by Farhad Matin Nafs. In this article, the author describes how information technology plays a pivotal role in developing the performance and success of virtual organizations, and information systems link and combine programmable product design and production with design and production process activities. To be. He also discusses the type of information technology needed for internal and external coordination.

Also, a study entitled "Study of customer relationship management system in the Iranian banking system" in 1389 by Alireza Shahraki; Mohsen Chehkandi and Alireza Mollashahi were performed. In this research, it has been tried to study the role of customer relationship management in Iranian banks and the weaknesses, strengths, goals as well as the effects of its implementation and the central role of the customer as a vital element for maintaining the bank. At the end, suggestions for improving the quality of services in the bank are presented.

Conceptual Model

According to research on the two concepts of customer relationship management and supply chain management, it has been found that research has examined each of these concepts in a company or organization separately, for example Shiri in 2009, he examined the relationship between product characteristics and supply chain strategy and used the performance criteria of a supply chain operational reference model as a decision criterion (Figure 24).

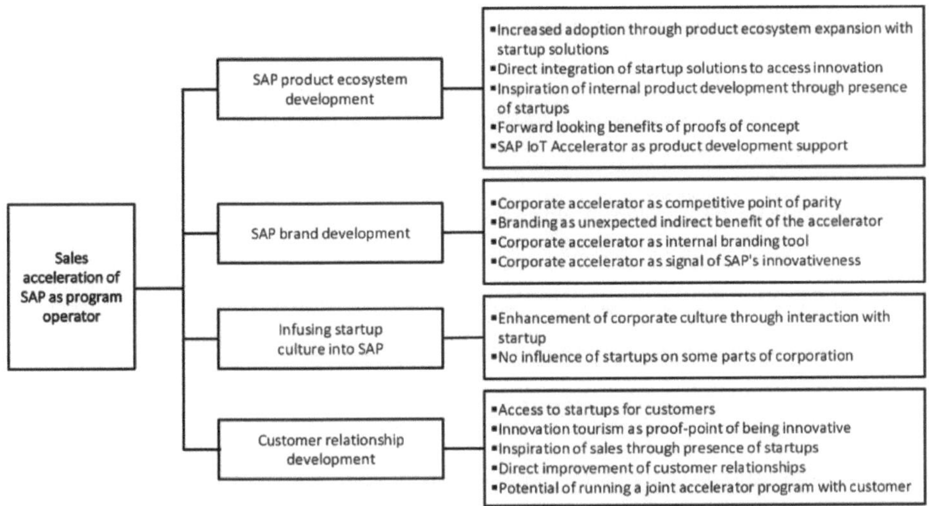

Figure 24. Sales acceleration of SAP as program operator

Also, Tabibi and Mazloumi (2009) have studied the scientific management structure with two prominent and major features of supply chain and strategic management. Jafarnejad et al. (2010) examine the need for production chain agility. In their view, for the ever-changing environment of this era, supply chain agility is a vital factor that affects the competitiveness of organizations. In order to create an agile supply chain, it is first necessary to clarify the meaning of agile supply chain.

Pouya (2005) examines the relationship between supply chain management and information technology support. Matin Nafs (2004) has dealt with the issue of how information technology plays a pivotal role in developing performance and reviewing the customer relationship management system in the Iranian banking system. Shahraki and try to study the role of customer relationship management in Iranian banks and the weaknesses, strengths, goals as well as the effects of its implementation and the central role of the customer as a vital element for maintaining the bank.

So far, no similar research has been conducted to examine the relationship between different dimensions of supply chain management and customer relationship management. The mutual dimensions of the mentioned concepts should be studied and studied.

Customer relationship management has four dimensions: customer retention and care, understanding customer needs, creating value for customers, customer orientation, customer orientation, and supply chain management in four dimensions: efficiency, integrity, accountability and trust. In this research, the interrelationship of the components of the conceptual model is studied.

The role of knowledge management in customer relationship

In today's knowledge-based economy, competitive advantage is increasingly found in facilitating information processes rather than in accessing specific resources and markets. Therefore, knowledge and intellectual capital are considered as the primary basis for achieving the main and strategic competencies for superior performance. In order to achieve sustainable competitive advantage, paying attention to existing knowledge, how to use it effectively and creating a structure for using new information and knowledge is considered important and vital that organizations should pay special attention to. Customer relationship management is one of the topics in today's global economy, which has led organizations to rethink their strategies for connecting with a wide range of customers and capturing this vast knowledge. But it can be boldly pointed out that effective communication with customers is not possible without the use of knowledge management. To increase the efficiency and effectiveness of the organization and ensure the optimal provision of goods and services to customers and their satisfaction, we must manage our knowledge of customers. Therefore, knowledge management is an integral part of customer relationship management. In this article, we intend to describe the role of knowledge management in customer relationship management. It is important that definitions of each of these concepts are provided before examining the role of knowledge management in customer relationship management to ensure that there is a common understanding of each.

Knowledge Management

In today's competitive market, characterized by uncertainty, companies have the ability to compete by creating, distributing, and transforming new knowledge into goods and services. In this way, knowledge creates a competitive advantage for the organization and allows the organization to solve problems and seize new opportunities. So knowledge will not only be a source of competitive advantage but will in fact be its only source. Knowledge management empowers, supports and strengthens the following functional and important elements: * Processes of discovering or building new knowledge and refining existing knowledge (creating knowledge inventory) * Knowledge sharing among individuals and at all organizational boundaries (knowledge flow management) * Creating and using knowledge as part of people's daily work and as part of decision making (applying knowledge) Knowledge management refers to the set of processes as a result of which knowledge is acquired, maintained and used, and its purpose is to exploit intellectual assets to increase productivity, create new values and increase competitiveness (Figure 25).

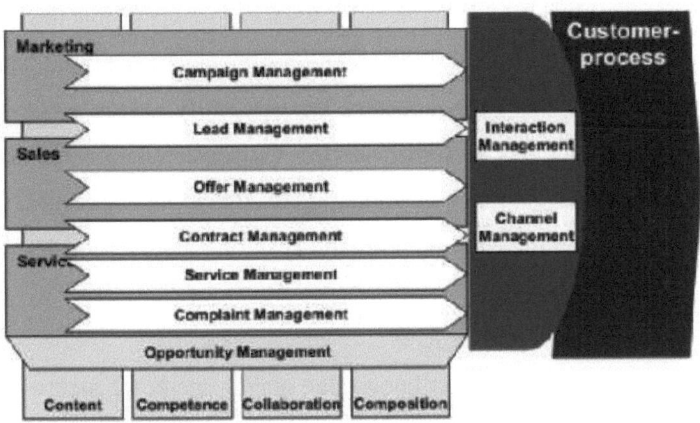

Figure 25. Customer Knowledge Management Model

Customer relation management

Customer Relationship Management (CRM), sometimes referred to as customer management, customer value management, customer-centric, or customer-centric management, has long been a common term for companies' desire to communicate one-on-one. In this regard, it can be acknowledged that companies that have succeeded in effectively attracting their customers, providing them with the desired services in the best way and retaining their best customers will have a positive impact on this in the end. They have seen their path to profitability. With the advent of e-commerce and new economic conditions, the development of stronger relationships with customers has become more important. CRM is a business strategy with the approach of establishing a lasting and long-term relationship with customers tailored to their circumstances and patterns of behavior that creates added value for both parties. CRM strategy is usually based on four executive goals:

1- Encourage customers of other companies or potential customers to make the first purchase from the company

2- Encourage customers who have made the first purchase to make subsequent purchases

3- Convert temporary customers to loyal customers

4- Providing highly desirable services for loyal customers so that they become the company's value. In fact, customer relationship management is all the processes and technologies that an organization has to identify, select, persuade, expand, maintain and employs customer service. Customer relationship management will enable managers to use customer knowledge to increase sales, service and development, and increase the profitability of ongoing relationships.

Knowledge flows in the CRM process

To embody the concept of customer knowledge management, we identify three types of knowledge flows that play a vital role in the interaction between the company and customers:

knowledge for, from and about the customer. In the first stage, to support customers in their purchasing cycle, a continuous flow of knowledge that is driven from company to customer (knowledge for the customer) is a prerequisite.

Knowledge for customers includes information about products, markets and suppliers. This dimension of knowledge also affects the customer's perception of service quality. At the same time, customer knowledge must be linked by the organization to create service and product innovation, generate ideas, and continually improve products and services. There are many ways to capture customer knowledge and involve customers in the innovation process.

For example, customers' knowledge of products, suppliers, and market trends can be used through an appropriate feedback mechanism to provide a systematic improvement and product innovation. Gathering and analyzing customer knowledge is definitely one of the oldest forms of KM in the field of CRM. In addition to raw customer data and past transactions, customer knowledge also takes into account current customer needs, future demands, communication, purchasing activity and financial ability. Customer knowledge is gathered in the CRM support and service process and analyzed in the CRM analysis process.

Customer Knowledge Management

At first glance, CKM may seem like just another name for CRM or KM. But in some respects, customer knowledge managers need a different approach than is common in KM and CRM. As a feature of CRM, customer relationship managers focus primarily on customer knowledge rather than customer knowledge. In other words, smart organizations have found that their customers are more aware of the employee who seeks knowledge through direct interaction with the customer as well as inquiring about customer knowledge from sales representatives.

Knowledge managers also focus on trying to transform employees from knowledge collectors to knowledge shareholders, usually through intranet-based knowledge sharing maps. In contrast, KM's exclusive focus on encouraging and strengthening productive and participatory relationships in line with the slogan "If we only knew what we know", CKM offers another dimension: "If we only knew what customers know" ». But why do customers want to share their knowledge to create value for the company and then pay for their knowledge developed in the company's products and services?

This is due to the change in attitudes towards customers as a knowledge institution. This change of attitude has a broad meaning. Most importantly, the customer is left with a passive recipient of products and services as was the case in traditional knowledge management. The customer is also freed from the shackles of the current CRM loyalty program chain. CKM also differs from traditional KM in the pursuit of goals. Considering that KM is looking for efficiency and profitability (avoiding wheel reinvention), CKM is in the direction of innovation and progress. Customer knowledge managers are looking for opportunities to partner with customers as co-creators of the organization's value. This is also evident in the willingness to maintain and cultivate the existing customer base in CRM.

Remember the famous CRM proverb that "retaining a customer is cheaper than finding it". Unfortunately, in a time when competitors' products, which are often imitations, are only a few clicks away from the customer, customer retention becomes extremely difficult. Because of this, customer knowledge managers are less concerned with customer retention. Instead, they focus on how the organization is developing and evolving by gaining new customers and engaging in active and value-added dialogue with them. How do customer knowledge managers create innovation and progress? As they have found, knowledge is not only present in employees but also in customers, which leads us to create value from innovation and progress, rather than cost savings in traditional KM.

Knowledge management facilitates integration between separate groups and departments in a customer relationship environment. These separate groups and divisions may be in different business units or geographical locations. Knowledge management facilitates a flow of knowledge around customer topics between workgroups, thereby integrating customer-related knowledge quickly and efficiently into achieving it. Knowledge management creates a vision for the customer regardless of the specialized field of application of the desired knowledge, the place where the knowledge is discovered or how to use it for the customer (Figure 26).

Categories of CK	Knowledge for customers	knowledge about customers	tacit knowledge conversion	knowledge from customers
Customer knowledge management process	Product features/benefits /identification	Customers' needs categorization	Market segmentation implementation	Segment needs pattern extraction
The Consumer Online Transaction Process	Information retrieval • Browsing • Gathering Information • Making product and price comparison • Learning about products and services	Information Transfer • Describing product prefrences • Registering • Providing feedback • Suplying private information		Product purchase • Providing credit card information • Providing actual product prefrences • Supplying payment and address information
CKM process in e-commerce	Providing effective information about producta and services using tools such as: e-catalogue, and intelligent agents and shopbot.	Gathering basic information about custemers and their needs through cookies, forms, web bugs, transaction log, spywares and click stream.	Manipulate customer data sources applying data mining thecniques, in order to extract useful knowlege about customers segments, potential market and needs in each segmen	Applying extracted knowelege from market to designe product and services and revising market strategies.

Figure 26. Customer Knowledge Management Framework in E-commerce

Knowledge management has a great impact on knowledge integration processes by clarifying the desired knowledge. Knowledge management has been very useful in cases where various functions in the organization prevent communication and knowledge circulation.

By recording customer knowledge and sharing it from a central point, it significantly increases the quality and speed of decision making and customer service. In a customer relationship management environment, participation is common and this is the result of expanding the organization's research and activities across geographical boundaries. These organizations use partnerships in a form of internal and external virtual communications to maintain the product, share, and power of customer knowledge. Technology knowledge management provides the organization with processes and contexts for participation, so that knowledge exchange sites are very secure in terms of technology provided using technology.

Knowledge management programs

Processes organize knowledge management systems in such a way that all the basic knowledge and sub-knowledge in the required fields are easily accessible and thus added value. Lead for the organization. Knowledge management provides employees with the tools, processes, and contexts to share knowledge based on customer needs. With the help of knowledge management, employees realize the value of customers' integrated knowledge, and through this, they can provide more complete services to more valuable customers. Therefore, knowledge management serves as a tool in the customer relationship management environment (Figure 27).

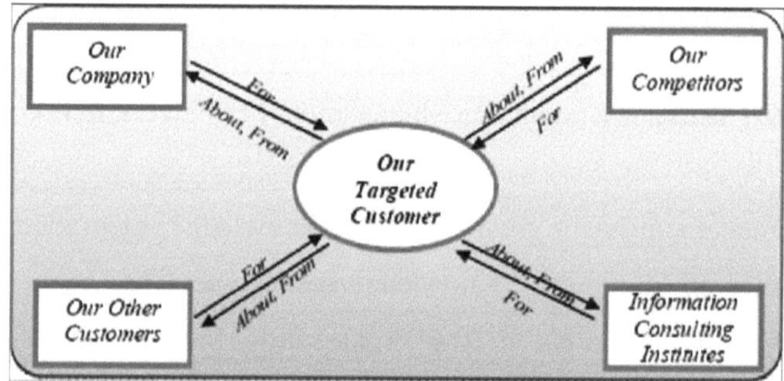

Figure 27. Quartet customer knowledge management model focusing on target customers

Knowledge management has been very useful in cases where various functions in the organization prevent communication and knowledge circulation. By recording customer knowledge and sharing it from a central point, it significantly increases the quality and speed of decision making and customer service. In a customer relationship management environment, participation is common and this is the result of expanding the organization's research and activities across geographical boundaries. These organizations use partnerships in the form of internal and external virtual communications to maintain the product, share, and influence of customer knowledge. Technology knowledge management provides the organization with processes and contexts for participation, so that knowledge-sharing neighborhoods are very secure in terms of technology provided using technology. Knowledge Management Processes Organize knowledge management systems in such a way that all the basic knowledge and sub-knowledge in the required fields are easily accessible and thus added value. Lead for the organization. Knowledge management provides employees with the tools, processes, and contexts to share knowledge based on customer needs. With the help of knowledge management, employees realize the value of customers' integrated knowledge, and through this, they can provide more complete services to more valuable customers. Therefore, knowledge management serves as a tool in the customer relationship management environment.

Looking at the above topics, it can be concluded that our expectation from customer knowledge management is to create the most value of knowledge and knowledge management at a strategic level.

Service marketers know that "having a customer" is important to service companies, not just customer acquisition. Research on customer presence shows that quality of service, quality of communication and overall satisfaction with services can enhance customer interaction by staying with a company.

We can use customer return management to prevent customers from switching service providers to other options. Customer return management aims to win over customers who have either been warned to end a business relationship or whose relationship has now ended. Customer return management ensures market profitability by adopting a specific management process including analysis, operation and control.

Obstacles and causes of customer relationship management system failure

Lack of commitment of senior managers to prioritize the customer relationship management system and institutionalize it in the organization; Lack of specialized and trained human resources in the field of customer relationship management; Insufficient allocation of financial resources; Inability to properly deal with organizational resistance; Weakness of database and information technology; Lack of support (presence of a support team, including manager and a number of experts, is essential to support CRM); Failure to delegate sufficient authority and restrict employee access to software for optimal use; Sufficient to CRM software and not institutionalizing and implementing customer relationship management at the organization level.

Chapter IV

Analysis of CRM

The two concepts of customer relationship management and supply chain management are important concepts in the field of management, striving to satisfy and provide products and services to customers quickly, product availability and maintaining profitability are the most important goals of manufacturing companies. Research has examined each of these concepts in a company or organization separately, as some researchers have examined the relationship between product features and supply chain strategy. Some researchers examine the need for production chain agility.

In their view, for the ever-changing environment of this era, supply chain agility is a vital factor that affects the competitiveness of organizations. So far, a similar study that examines the interrelationship between different dimensions of supply chain management and customer relationship management has not been conducted in the present study. Structural equations of interrelationship between the dimensions of the mentioned concepts should be studied and studied. Customer relationship management has five dimensions: customer retention and care, understanding customer needs, creating value for customers, customer-centric, customer-oriented, and supply chain management consists of four dimensions of efficiency, integrity, accountability and trust.

Based on the findings, it was found that understanding customer needs as one of the dimensions of customer relationship management has a significant relationship with the two variables of trust and integrity. It was also found that with increasing the degree of integration in supply chain management, the level of understanding of customer needs increases. Also, customer retention as one of the dimensions of customer relationship management has a significant relationship with the two variables of trust and integrity. That is, with increasing trust in supply chain management, the amount of customer retention and care increases.

There is also a strong positive relationship between the two variables of integration and customer retention, ie with increasing the level of integration in supply chain management, the amount of customer retention and care increases. The results showed that creating value for the customer as one of the dimensions of customer relationship management has a significant relationship with the two variables of efficiency and integration. That is, with increasing efficiency in supply chain management, the amount of value creation for the customer increases.

And with increasing integration in supply chain management, the amount of value creation for the customer increases. The results also show that customer orientation as one of the dimensions of customer relationship management has a significant relationship with the three variables of trust, accountability and integration. That is, with increasing trust in management, the supply chain increases the amount of customer orientation. Customer orientation also increases with increasing responsiveness in supply chain management. Finally, with the improvement of integration in supply chain management, the level of customer orientation increases. Examination of the collected data shows that customer-centric as one of the dimensions of customer relationship management has a significant relationship with the three variables of trust, accountability and integration, so that with increasing trust in management, customer-centric supply chain increases. By improving the level of responsiveness in supply chain management, the amount of customer-centricity increases.

Also, with the increase of integration in supply chain management, the amount of customer orientation increases. On the other hand, the results show that there is a significant relationship between trust and value creation and efficiency of understanding customer needs, efficiency and customer retention, efficiency and customer orientation, efficiency and customer orientation, responsiveness and value creation, customer responsiveness and retention, responsiveness and understanding of needs does not have.

Therefore, it is clear that among the supply chain management factors, integration factor is considered as the most important variable affecting customer relationship management, the reason for this is the significant impact of this variable on all aspects of customer relationship management. Then the trust variable is effective on four dimensions of customer relationship management and accountability has a positive effect on customer orientation and customer orientation and finally the efficiency of supply chain management can affect the creation of value to the company's customers.

All the variables described and the relationships between them are direct, which is mutually improved by the reinforcement and optimization of each of them. For example, increasing trust in supply chain management improves customer retention and care. Therefore, different dimensions of customer relationship management and supply chain management simultaneously affect each other and strengthen each other. Due to the lack of similar research on the relationship between supply chain management and customer relationship management as discussed in the present study, the results obtained cannot be compared with the results of other studies. However, the obtained results can be compared with other research results as a scientific and research finding in future research.

CRM Business Advantages

By focusing on the most profitable customers and also caring for the customers who are less profitable for you, using the most efficient methods, your profitability will increase. Although using a customer management system can be costly and time consuming for the company, it will also have potential benefits. The most important advantage of using a CRM system is better communication with existing customers, which leads to the following achievements:

- Increase sales through proper timing (by predicting customer needs based on a review of customer history history)
- Better identification of customer needs by recognizing the specific needs of each customer
- Selling a product along with other products by offering and offering complementary and alternative products
- Determine whether each customer is profitable or not This will lead to better marketing of your products and services, provided that targeted and effective marketing is focused on the needs of customers and also the creation of new or updated products and services in order to gain a better market and business in the future.

Ultimately, these can lead to the following results for your organization:

> Increase customer satisfaction and retention and ensure that your company's reputation will be preserved and your market will continue to grow.

> It will add value to existing customers, and the costs you incur to connect and support them will be reduced by increasing overall efficiency and reducing the cost of goods sold.

> By focusing on the most profitable customers and also caring for the customers who are less profitable for you, using the most efficient methods, your profitability will increase.

Possible obstacles to the customer relationship management system

There are several reasons for using a customer relationship management system method and how using this method leads to our desired results. There is always the possibility that there is a lack of commitment among individuals to follow the methods and principles of the customer relationship management system. Adapting to customer-centric approaches sometimes requires cultural change. There is always the risk that customer relationships will lead to disruptions and problems unless all members and activists of the company do their best to examine their behaviors from a customer perspective. In this case, the result will not be anything other than customer dissatisfaction and consequent loss of profitability. Poor communication with the customer can lead to a reduction in purchases. In order to make your customer relationship management system more efficient, all of your staff need to know enough about the information you need and how to use it. Poor communication can cause problems in the implementation patterns of various communication management methods. Management responsibilities for creating customer orientation in any project are practically the responsibility of management. If one of the suggested templates is not suitable for your customers, do not implement it. And send your team to find a workable and efficient solution.

CRM technology market

The four major companies that sell customer relationship management (CRM) systems are Salesforce.com, Microsoft, SAP and Oracle. The other companies that offer this product are more well-known among the smaller businesses, but these four brands are the choice of the larger companies.

CRM systems that are implemented within the company are responsible for managing, controlling, securing, and maintaining information and data within the company. With this approach, the buyer pre-purchases all licenses instead of paying an annual subscription. This software is installed on the company's main server and the user must pay the installation fee and all updates. Companies with sophisticated CRM systems benefit the most from launching this software.

Cloud-based CRMs, also known as SaaS (Licensed Software), are installed on remote external networks, and employees can access the Internet at any time, from anywhere, and sometimes from anywhere. Access them through a service provider who oversees installation and maintenance.

The relatively fast speed and deployment of cloud-based software is useful for companies with little expertise in technology. Many companies may prefer this method because it is low cost. Sellers such as Salesforce.com offer subscribers the option of paying monthly or annually for their cloud computing services. The most important concern of companies that use cloud-based systems is data security.

This concern is due to the fact that these companies do not directly control the database. If the company providing the cloud computing service goes bankrupt or is acquired by another company, the data may become problematic or even lost. Costs can also be a concern for them, as subscription costs for software may be more expensive than in-house models. Open-source customer relationship management (CRM) programs make their code available to the public, allowing companies to make the necessary changes at no cost. Open-source CRM systems also allow data changes to be connected to social media channels, thus helping companies improve their social CRM activities. In the open-source software market, SugarCRM is a good choice. Which method of CRM installation the company uses depends on the business needs, resources and goals, and of course each of these options has different costs.

Customer Relationship Management (CRM) Challenges

Despite all the advances in customer relationship management technology, without proper management, the CRM system can be nothing more than a repository where customer information is stored. The data should be organized on a regular basis so that users can easily access the information they need. Also, because different data is organized in an interface or dashboard, companies have to work hard to get an overview of the customer and related data. Challenges arise when customer information is stored in separate systems or data is duplicated and outdated.

This causes business processes to be hampered or slowed down. These problems lead to long waiting times during telephone calls, reduced customer recognition, and inefficient technical support. Studies show that customers, especially those belonging to the millennial generation, are extremely dissatisfied with the performance of communication centers. They tend to connect with the company through wider communication channels.

Channels such as smartphone apps, web chat and of course social media. The main challenge of a customer relationship management (CRM) system is to provide an inter-channel experience that is consistent and reliable. For example, social media is recognized as the most useful of these channels, and customers can use it to access companies, ask questions, solve problems, and not have to spend hours in the traditional way on the phone or waiting for an answer via email.

In some cases, especially in cases where there is a lot of contact and close contact with customers, social media cannot respond to proper customer service. Companies are also still struggling to identify potential customers. Newer generation technologies that integrate CRM data with other data from companies such as Dunn & Bradstreet have also emerged to help sales and marketing teams find more potential customers. The best performance of these methods is when companies organize their current data and delete incomplete and duplicate records before completing their system with new data and information.

Using the right tools and technologies can be a great way to meet most of the challenges that business sales managers face. Instead of trying hard and time-consuming solutions, try to use a simple solution to run the sales process and solve the challenges ahead. For example, customer relationship management can help you create and track sales, can lead to repeat sales to your customers, manage sales team tasks and measure the performance of your employees, you know to promote and lead the sales team How to act. Because CRM transfers customer information from marketing to sales and customer service, your marketing and sales team knows more about your customers and is more effective in increasing customer value and customer loyalty.

Why do businesses need social CRM?

Social CRM allows a business to communicate with customers using its chosen channels, ie by phone, text, chat, email or social media (for example, Facebook or Twitter). Behind these interactions, a social CRM software helps businesses gain a deeper insight into how customers feel about their company, their brand, and their particular products or services. The best CRM software is able to use this customer profile dynamically and use it by publishing information in different teams including customer service, marketing and sales.

Use social CRM for customer service

Social CRM is used by companies to optimize service levels and multi-channel customer experience. Social CRM can help businesses deliver customer service seamlessly and seamlessly, so that it is customer-friendly. Consumers today expect great service from a business regardless of their communication channel. Consumers expect to be able to easily change their communication channels and be responsive to the business they want quickly and personally in each of them.

If the business can remember them, then they do not have to re-introduce themselves in any connection with the system. This is especially important because customers are increasingly using social media as the easiest way to express their desires. Many companies get their customer feedback from Twitter.

With social CRM, when a customer decides to connect with a business through a social channel, this interaction can be tracked and managed in more detail because a traditional CRM software can be a phone message or email Follow.

Use of social CRM in marketing

Social CRM helps businesses turn customer engagement into a two-way street. Customers become part of a brand's story instead of a passive audience, and in turn, they can see the value of a brand as a customer. A marketing team may produce great content - blogs, Facebook posts, YouTube videos, Instagram accounts and engaging tweets, but this is a one-way conversation. Social CRM can help businesses identify and reward brand fans and influencers, and encourage them to define and describe your brand. In one survey, 89% of respondents said that social media increased their brand visibility, while nearly half reported that spending 6 hours a week on social media reduced their public marketing costs.

Use social CRM in sales management

Tracking customers in the sales funnel can be done using social CRM. Sales teams can create a personalized experience for their users instead of using the traditional CRM approach. Beyond personalization, sales teams can increase their sales by using good compliments and descriptions from their customers on social media. In a Salesforce customer survey, 55% reported increased customer loyalty and 54% increased sales revenue.

What are the benefits of social CRM?

For marketing, sales, and customer service units, social CRM can help potential customers become satisfied customers and be ambassadors for introducing and defining an organization's brand and branding.

Key benefits of social CRM

1- Providing support and services to the customer in the social networks used by them

2- Interact and communicate with customers in real time

3- Monitor and solve problems quickly by monitoring and following social networks

4- Find and reward brand sponsors and customers who help others

5- Most brands are seen in places where audiences spend their time

6- Increase interaction and deep relationships with customers

References

1- Bashiri, M., 2001, A model for measuring customer satisfaction and its application in standard audits, Master Thesis in Industrial Engineering, Tarbiat Modares University.

2- Pouya Alireza (2005); "Supply Chain Management and Information Technology Support", Tadbir Monthly - Year 15 - No. 145.

3- Jafarnejad Ahmad; Humiliating Ali; Darwish Maryam; Yasai Mehrdad; (2010) "Presenting a method for measuring supply chain agility using a combination of graph theory, matrix approach and fuzzy logic" Quarterly Journal of Business Research, No. 54, Spring 2010.

4- George P. Kachen and Martin E. Larry Weir, translated by Nowruzizadeh; Turning the supply chain into a revenue chain; New Thoughts, Selected Management Monthly, Issue 8, July 2001, Pages 5 to 7.

5- Hamid Reza Charmchi; The concept of supply chain in industry and its benefits; Industry Quarterly; No. 23; Summer 79; Pages 6 to 9.

6- Mehdi Ghazanfari, Afshin Riyazi, Massoud Kazemi; Supply chain management; Journal of Tadbir; No. 117; Aban 80 pages 20 to 27.

7- Dehghanizadeh, Mohammad, Haji Ali Akbari, Reza, (2005), Customer Relationship Management, Skills Monthly, No. 47, pp. 36-28.

8- Ranjbar, Mokhtar, Ahmadinejad, Arman, (2003), The position of customer relationship management in relational marketing, Advertising Knowledge, No. 24, pp. 36-31.

9- Rahnamood, F., "Empowering Employees, a Step Towards Customer Orientation", Development Management Process, No. 56, 2004. Thirteenth year; Management knowledge; No. 59, Winter 79 and pp. 137-135 to 142.

10- Soleimani Shiri Gholam Hossein; (2009), Presenting a Multi-Criteria Decision Model for Selecting the Best Suppliers in the Supply Chain by Combining Analytic Hierarchy Process and Ideal Planning (Case Study of Automotive Industry) Source: Management Quarterly, Year 6, Issue 15, Winter 2009.

11- Shah Samandi, Parasto, Data Mining in Customer Relationship Management, Tadbir, Vol. 156, 2005.

12- Salehi Sedghiani, Jamshid, Akhavan, Maryam, (2004), Customer Relationship Management, Journal of Development and Management, No. 176, pp. 36-24.

13- Medical Mohammad Reza; A rare oppressed person; (2009) "Presenting a model for analysis, selection and implementation of business supply chain strategy" Iranian Journal of Management Sciences Quarterly, Fourth Year, No. 16, Winter 2009.

14- Ali Akbar Saeedi Kia, Jafar Motahari Fard, Mohammad Tahir Riyazi; Supply chain management; Journal of Methods; Tenth year; Issue 61.

15- Gholamian, Mohammad Reza, Khajeh Afzali, Maryam, Ebrahimi, Babak, (2006), Knowledge Management in Customer Relationships, Tadbir Monthly, No. 176, pp. 29-22.

16- Farzi, Hossein, (2007), Customer Relationship Management, Skills Monthly, No. 56, pp. 29-26.

17- Ghorbani, Alireza, (2009). Comparison of various customer relationship management technologies in order to create value for customers of banks in Guilan province. Master Thesis, Department of Business Management, Islamic Azad University, Rasht Branch.

18- Mortazavi, Mohammad Reza, (2003). Factors influencing the development of information systems. Master Thesis, Department of Industrial Engineering, Faculty of Engineering, Tarbiat Modares University.

19- Maurice Cohen et al., Saturn Supply Chain Innovation; Superior value in after-sales service; Translated by Dr. Abdolreza Rezainejad; Selected Management Monthly, No. 4, February 79, pp. 75-82.

20- Mahdavi Nia, Mohammad, Ghodratpour, Behrooz, (2005), Applying CRM Customer Relationship Management to Increase Sales and Retain Customers of Insurance Companies, Asia Quarterly, pp. 26-21.

21- Milton, Asri, Industrial Accounting (Planning and Control), translated by Farshid Navisi ... (and others), Volume II, Nineteenth Edition, Auditing Organization, 2005.

22- Niknia, Babak, (2007), Customer Relationship Management (CRM), Shoe Industry, Fourteenth Year, No. 118, pp. 54-52.

23- Elahi, Sh., Heidari, B, first edition, 2005, customer relationship management, publishing and commercial publishing.

24- An exploratory study of implementation of customer relationship management strategy, 2007, Business process management journal, Sweden, Aihie Osarenkhoe.

25- Andreas Reichhart and Matthias Holweg, creating customer responsive supply chain, A Reconciliation of concepts, judge business school.

26- Burnett, K. (2001); Handbook of key Customer Relationship Management; The Definitive Guide to winning, managing and Developing key Account business; Prentice Hall: New Jersy.

27- Chalmeta, R., Grangel, R. (2005). Performance measurement systems for virtual enterprise integration, Computer Integrated Manufacturing, PP 73-84.

28- Curry, J., Curry, A., (2000). The customer marketing method: How to implement and profit from customer Relation Management, free press.

29- Dimitris N.Chorafas, Integrating erp, crm, supply chain management and smar material, Auerbach, 2001, CRC press, page69.

30- driven supply network –integrating crm & scm, University of Augsburg, page3-7.

31- Gaining customer knowledge through analytical CRM, 2005, Industrial management & data systems, UK, Mark Xu.

32- Gary, Paul & Jungbok Byun (2001); Customer Relationship Management; University of California; Available at L <www.criso.edu> (07, 09, 2004).

33- Greenberg. paul; CRM at the speed of light, third edition: Essential Customer strategies, McGraw Hill, 2004.

34- Halbreat J, & Rogers, T, (1999); Customer Relationship Management; a Leadership and motivation model for the twenty - first country business; the TQM magazine. Volume 11 NO3 pp.161-171.

35- Osarenkoe, Aihie, Bennani, Az-Eddine, (2007). An exploratory Study of implementation of Customer, Business Process Management Journal, Vol. 13 No. 1, PP.139-164.

36- Park, C., Kim, Y., (2003), Frame work of dynamic CRM: Linking marketing with information strategy, business Process management, PP52-68.

37- Payne and Frow; Definition of CRM and Classification of CRM; 2005.

38- Seift R. S (2001): Accelerating Customer Relationship wring CRM and technologies; Prentice Hall: New Jersy.

39- Strauss, J., Frost, R., (2002). Customer relationship management, Emarketing, Second ed. Prentice Hall, Newyourk.

40- Tanoury D, Ireland K; Why CRM Projects fail: Common Strategic & Tactical Mistakes, ITtoolbox CRM, 2002.

41- Teo, Devadoss, Paul, (2006). Towards a holistic perspective of Customer Relationship Management (CRM) implementation: A Case Study of the Housing and Development Board, Singapore, Decision Support Systems, Vol. 42, PP. 1213-1229.

42- Teo, T., Pan, S., (2006). Towards a holistic perspective of customer relationship management (CRM) implementation: A case study of the Housing and Development Board, singapore, Decision support systems. PP 1-15.

43- Teo, T., (2000). Management issues in data warehousing: insights from the Housing and Development Board, Decision support systems.

44- The design, implementation and monitoring of a CRM program: a case study, 2004, Marketing Intelligence & planning, Netherlands, Adam Leendgreen.

45- Winer, R.S. (2001). A framework for customer relationship management, California management reviw 43 (4). PP 89-105.

46- Yun E. Zeng and H. Joseph Wen and David C. Yen; Customer relationship management (CRM) in business-to-business (B2B) e-commerce; MCB UP Ltd, 2003, pages: 39 – 44.

More
Books!

OMNIScriptum

Printed by Books on Demand GmbH, Norderstedt / Germany